TRISKEL TWO

Triskel Two

Essays on Welsh and Anglo-Welsh Literature

Editors
SAM ADAMS
and
GWILYM REES HUGHES

CHRISTOPHER DAVIES

First published in 1973
by Christopher Davies (Publishers) Ltd.
Llandybie, Carmarthenshire,
and printed by
The Salesbury Press
Llandybie, Carmarthenshire.

SBN 7154 0046 0

Published with the support of the Welsh Arts Council.

CONTENTS

Introduction

The essays in this volume were all specially commissioned and none have been previously published. They provide assessments of writers and their work based upon careful textual study and, though no major revaluations result, much new light is cast upon themes, techniques and developments.

The contributions on Welsh language writers include Elan Class Stephens's balanced assessment of the poetry of Dr. Gwyn Thomas and R. Gerallt Jones's measured appreciation of the poetry of Sir T.H. Parry-Williams, the most illustrious member of a small but brilliant coterie of writers whose work exercised a profound influence on the course of Welsh literature during the first half of the twentieth century. Dr. J. Gwyn Griffiths contributes a study in depth of Dr. Pennar Davies, regarded by many as one of the most exciting poets writing in Wales today, while Dr. Davies himself (almost equally well-known as a critic) provides a new estimate of the plays of Saunders Lewis.

David Shayer's essay on the poetry of Alun Lewis adds very considerably to the store of information available about a poet, neglected of late, whose breadth of intellect and passionate response to the human predicament deserve far wider recognition. There is no danger of Dylan Thomas being neglected, but there has been a tendency for critics to concentrate on the early poems, sometimes dismissing the later work entirely. Here, however, John Ackerman, whose book on Thomas is one of the most reliable studies available, shows how the consistency in his themes and imagery extends to the final, uncompleted 'In country sleep'. Leslie Norris, editor of the Faber memorial volume *Vernon Watkins 1906-1967* provides a further study of that other Swansea poet. He is, like Roland Mathias who wrote on Watkins for *Triskel One*, eminently qualified by his long study of and continued enthusiasm for Watkins's work and by being himself a poet. Surveys of Anglo-Welsh prose are few and far between. Dr. Glyn Tegai Hughes's lucid and fascinating history of the development of the mythology of the mining valleys is, therefore, particularly valuable as an introduction to a field in which there is still so much work to be done.

As in *Triskel One*, we have presented critical studies of Welsh and Anglo-Welsh literature together, to reflect the contemporary co-existence in Wales of two distinct but overlapping cultures, each with its own literary past and present. As a whole the book may be seen as an expression of the belief that the artistic future of Wales lies in bilingualism, for (as Professor Gwyn Jones has written) 'the preservation and extension of the Welsh language are of primary importance to Anglo-Welsh literature' and equally the Welsh language writer, so long as he maintains a sturdy independence of spirit, can and does benefit from the enormous wealth and diversity of literature in English.

Sam Adams

Gwilym Rees Hughes

THE ROLE OF NATURE IN THE POETRY
OF DYLAN THOMAS

John Ackerman

As might be expected, the most useful and illuminating insights into a poet's work are usually provided by the poet himself; and in this respect Dylan Thomas's letters, a rich and energetic commentary on his life and writing where the vivacity of language never fails whatever the urgent personal problems being aired, may be compared with those of Keats. They are in themselves a wholly original and distinctive part of the writer's oeuvre. Additional guidelines for understanding the poetry have been provided by Thomas in his broadcasts, replies to questionnaires, and book reviews.

Generally, these remarks emphasise the importance of the sound and the *physical* impact of poetry. It is not simply a matter of the traditional use of sound in poetry as part of its effect. Thomas was speaking of something more than, and beyond this; and it leads to a vital aspect of his originality (too often mistaken by critics in the early years—and still by some hostile to the kind of poetry he writes—as wanton obscurity, an inability to attain intellectual clarity). And though Dylan Thomas's poetry shows important developments in theme and technique, this essential feature of his writing whereby the physical quality of thought and feeling is recorded remains its dominant characteristic. The verbal energy and purpose derive from:

9

– the strong. stressing of the physical. Nearly all my images, coming, as they do, from my solid and fluid world of flesh and blood, are set out in terms of their progenitors.[1]

Emphasising as it does the sensory power of words, and in this respect uniquely re-vitalising the language in his time (c.f. Keats's 'English ought to be kept up' , the verbal links are less intellectual, logical, and syntactical, than rhythmically determined and built upon a syllabic and alliterative structure. Such a poetry has its own disciplines; that they are not primarily intellectual or conceptual does not imply their absence. Relatedly, meaning in his verse, to a greater extent than is usual in poetry, is in terms of affective and sensory perception. It holds true that Thomas introduced us, in this way, to new modes of thinking and feeling in his verse.[3]

Notably, in an early letter, Thomas writes that it is through the physical body that man apprehends the world around him:

All thoughts and actions emanate from the body. Therefore the description of a thought or action — however abstruse it may be — can be beaten home by bringing it onto a physical level. Every idea, intuitive or intellectual, can be imaged and translated in terms of the body, its flesh, skin, blood, sinews, veins, glands, organs, cells or senses.[4]

Clearly this has profound and significant influence on Thomas's choice and handling of themes. Informing their evolution and presentation, it determines, for example, the ways in which his poetry is concerned with conveying the instinctive, the intuitional and, increasingly, the mystical in man and his relationship with the natural world: such as in the re-discovery of childhood vision in 'Fern Hill', 'Poem on his birthday''s affirmation of faith in man's unity with other creatures and the whole of the natural world despite the ubiquity of death, the evocation of nature's benevolence in 'In country sleep', in the view of death as final union with nature in 'A Refusal to Mourn the Death, by Fire, of a Child in London' and the more personal and poignant registering of this in 'Elegy'.

Stressing the manner in which man is rooted in the earth, an essentially physical being - and this of course does not imply only limitations - Thomas emphasises in the same letter that

> The body, its appearance, death, and disease, is a fact, sure as the fact of a tree. It has its roots in the same earth as the tree. The greatest description I know of our own 'earthiness' is to be found in John Donne's Devotions, where he describes man as earth of the earth, his body earth, his hair a wild shrub growing out of the land.[5]

Consequently Thomas's concept of poetry, and of man's relation to it, suggesting as it does the pre-eminence of physical and sensory perception, implies, and this is perhaps the major theme in his verse, an organic link between man and the natural world. And in Thomas nature is always seen as an organic power, not simply as a source of metaphor as is usually the case in Yeats or Eliot. Again, in contrast to Hopkins, for whom nature is emblematic of God and *is* God's grandeur in the world. for Thomas nature is important because of its vital link with man.

Nature, then, is the creative and dynamic force operating in the physical world, his sense of indissoluble unity with which Thomas registers in his earliest poems (though at this stage characteristically emphasising the processes of death and destruction man also shares with nature):

> *The force that through the green fuse drives the flower*
> *Drives my green age; that blasts the roots of trees*
> *Is my destroyer . . .*

11

The Force that drives the water through the rocks
Drives my red blood; that dries the mouthing streams
Turns mine to wax.

In the light of Thomas's earlier insistence that it is
through the physical body that man apprehends all forms of
experience, re-iterated later in the same letter:

Through my small, bonebound island I have learnt all
I know, experienced all, and sensed all. All I write is insep-
arable from the island . . . [6]

it is not surprising that the relationship of his own body to
the world of nature is a major preoccupation.

In a related way, he suggests in 'When all my five and
country senses see' that visionary experience (including the
poetic [7]) is attained through improvement of sensory perception [8] : that is, essentially physical perception, natural
('country') as opposed to spiritual or moral, in this profoundly anti-spiritual poem. At death and the body's diss-
olution when 'five eyes break', it is a love whose roots are
sensual that survives, witnessed and celebrated in other
lovers; the continuing sensual vision (born from and learned
through the senses in contrast, for example, to Eliot's asens-
ory and abstract revelation) implied in man's biological
continuum:

My one and noble heart has witnesses
In all love's countries, that will grope awake;
And when blind sleep drops on the spying senses,
The heart is sensual, though five eyes break.

Significantly, and relatedly, in 'And death shall have no
dominion' 'salvation is not by faith ('Faith in their hands
shall snap in two') but by nature' [9] :

Heads of the characters hammer through daisies

a poetic statement of 'pushing up the daisies', the colloquial expression no less *simpliste* than the equally familiar 'in heaven'. Aware of the importance of nature in this poem Tindall has rightly observed that 'here, as elsewhere in Thomas, Christian references are analogies for natural event or condition',[10] — for the Bible remained one of Thomas's main sources of metaphor and myth.

In the early poetry Thomas explores the unity between man and nature, mainly in terms of his own body, with a concentration on such processes as conception, birth, sexuality and death. Indeed at times his sense of individual identity seems about to be overwhelmed by his sense of the forces of nature, of which his single body is but a part, though such lines as:

> *Today, this insect, and the world I breathe,*
> *Now that my symbols have outelbowed space*

image his poetry as extending his world beyond the microcosm of his own body (the 'insect').

Undoubtedly a major development in Thomas's poetry is his achievement of an externalised vision of the unity between man and nature, and its increasingly mystical implications as in 'Elegy' and 'In the white giant's thigh'. A poem that shows the wider vision of man's final reabsorption into natural life is 'A Refusal to Mourn . . .' This refusal is based on the fact that the child, like Wordsworth's 'Lucy' has rejoined 'earth's diurnal course/ With rocks, and stones, and trees'[11]:

> *Robed in the long friends*
> *The grains beyond age, the dark veins of her mother*

In his interesting study *Religious Trends in English Poetry* (vol. V1, 1920-1965) H.N. Fairchild has stated that 'despite all its Christian images, Thomas's 'A Refusal to

Mourn the Death, by Fire, of a Child in London' is more loyal to traditional romantic pantheism than Jeffer's poem. It affirms the unity of all creatures, human and nonhuman, living and dead, with death as a return to holy, hidden germs of life in water and corn.'[12] Yet Dylan Thomas has gone beyond nineteenth century romantic pantheism, as represented by Wordsworth, and re-cast for our own time this belief in, and sense of ultimate return to nature. Unlike the passivity of Wordsworth's lines:

> *No motion has she now, no force;*
> *She neither hears nor sees;*

Thomas's view of this return suggests the shared energy of this re-absorption (it is *there* in the renewed vigour and resurgence of the last stanza):

> *Secret by the unmourning water*
> *Of the riding Thames.*

Nor is it a momentary drifting into such faith ('A slumber did my spirit seal'[13]) but a sustained and argued belief related to the mythopoeic concept of man's relationship to nature built up in the rest of the poet's work.

I have already suggested that Thomas wished to re-create in a physical and direct way in his poetry the experiences that were the subject matter of his verse, and one recalls, in this respect, Vernon Watkins's revealing comment that 'out of a lump of texture or nest of phrases he created music, testing everything by physical feeling'![14] Readers are no doubt already familiar with the importance of nature in the poetry of childhood, and it is the ecstatic quality of recollection in 'Fern Hill' and 'Poem in October', produced by an irresistible rhythmic spell and an emotive and sensuous use of word and image stunningly sustained, that distinguishes these poems. The visionary experience is there to be shared if we are emotionally and sensuously alive enough to register the impact:

> *And I saw in the turning so clearly a child's*
> *Forgotten mornings when he walked with his mother*
> *Through the parables*
> *Of sunlight*
> *And the legends of the green chapels*
> *And the twice told fields of infancy*
> *That his tears burned my cheeks and his heart moved in*
> *mine.*

Again, Biblical images ('parables', 'chapels') are used as metaphor to convey the joy and (for the child) eternity of the natural world. One recalls Thomas's later attempt in 'In country sleep' to establish a more permanent sense of this joy and eternal goodness in nature (once more borrowing Biblical metaphor in 'holy', and with a pun on the word 'God'):

> *The country is holy: O bide in that country kind,*
> *Know the green good,*

It seems invidious to select an isolated instance from 'Fern Hill', a poem of unbroken visionary landscapes, an immediately physical 'golden world' of nature flowing about the farm:

> *And honoured among wagons I was prince of the apple*
> *towns*
> *And once below a time I lordly had the trees and leaves*
> *Trail with daisies and barley*
> *Down the rivers of the windfall light.*

Thomas's own comments, again in his letters, on Wordsworth's pantheism are of considerable comparative interest. It is against this achieved poetry of vision, and bearing in mind what Dylan Thomas was trying to do in his poems, that we may set his youthful, perhaps callow and unfair but not entirely unilluminating dismissal of Wordsworth's pantheism in a letter written when he was eighteen:

> He writes about mysticism but he is not a mystic; he describes what mystics have been known to feel, but he himself doesn't feel anything . . . He could well have written his Ode in the form of a treatise: 'Mysticism and its Relations to the Juvenile Mind'.

It is in the last poems, which spring from the seascapes and rural settings of Laugharne and the Carmarthenshire countryside, that Thomas's absorption with nature moves to full realisation. H.N.Fairchild observes that 'his later work tends to be richer in happy nature-images drawn from his boyhood than are the earlier 'womb-tomb' poems. The effort to remember rather than to dream was part of that emergence from darkness into light which he thought essential to his growth as a poet'[16] and this points, though in some respects in a superficial way, to crucial aspects of Thomas's development. I think there were three important factors in the poet's deepening and extending of his vision: the impact of war; the return to Wales and its landscapes; a third, I suspect, was his selling of the early Notebooks in 1941, which marked a decisive break with his poetry of adolescence. It was a break of which Thomas, again his own best critic, was vividly aware:

> It's lovely when you burn your boats. They burn so beautifully.

Fitzgibbon has acutely observed that 'Those notebooks were his youth, those notebooks were his poems, those notebooks were Dylan the young poet'.[18] No longer was there the inspiration and example to return to his own introspective world. His obsession with the mortality of his own body became the wider, calmer sense of a doom shared with natural life in 'the bent bay's grave' as he perceived:

Herons walk in their shroud.

The Laugharne sea-scape, a shared grave, becomes the one world of man and nature on their voyage to death in 'Poem on his birthday', 'Over Sir John's Hill', 'Author's Prologue'. And the absorption of the poet in this world becomes the main inspiration of his themes and imagery: while the 'small, bonebound island' of the poet reaches the wider vision of 'The mansouled fiery islands'.

Speaking of his solitary absorption in Laugharne, as he worked in his cliff-side shed overlooking the bay and the surrounding countryside, or walked the winding path down to the village, Caitlin Thomas writes of him at the time of composition of these last poems:

> So he was much better than me at contenting himself with the very simple . . . life.Because, there is no other possible explanation, he lived in a world of his own: 'out of this world'.[19]

And reading the poems one has the sense of a man communing most deeply with the life of nature— a world whose reality (in contrast to the American lecture tours and adopted role of entertainer) immediately surrounded and profoundly absorbed him:

In his house on stilts high among beaks
And palavers of birds . . .

Under and round him go
Flounders, gulls, on their cold, dying trails . . .

17

In the thistledown fall,
He sings towards anguish; finches fly
In the claw tracks of hawks
On a seizing sky . . .

Significantly, in his 'Prologue' to the *Collected Poems,* he builds in his poetry the ark of his love that man and beast may enter.

I would like, in conclusion, to show related aspects of the role of nature in these later poems. Bearing in mind Thomas's comment on the static element in Wordsworth's poetry, a criticism implied and extended in the same letter (the prejudiced and partial view of course of another poet but focussing Thomas's own creative process):

> He hadn't a spark of mysticism in him . . . And mysticism is illogical, unintellectual, and dogmatic . . . the (Wordsworth) platitudinary reporter of Nature in her dullest moods

clearly Thomas already grasped the nonrational aspect of mystical experience. This criticism also highlights Thomas's concern to present nature in terms of heightened sensory perception, usually crystallised in the moment of visionary experience. In this kind of poetry the concept of time is important, and his introduction to his broadcast reading of the poems that were to form part of the longer sequence 'In Country Heaven',[21] holds a fascinating and crucial comment on his view of time:

> The remembered tellings, which are the components of the poem, are not all told as though they are remembered; the poem will not be a series of poems in the past tense. The memory, in all tenses can look towards the future, can caution and admonish. The rememberer may live himself back into active participation in the remembered scene, adventure, or spiritual condition.[22]

This concept of times directs Thomas's presentation of

nature; from it derives the importance of physical immediacy, the actuality evoked by the affective and sensuous
impact of image and rhythm, resulting in 'active partic-
ipation', though the poem may be one of recollection,
prophecy, or divination. Thus in 'A Winter's Tale', which is
an expansive and lyrical evocation of country life in winter:

> *And the stars falling cold,*
> *And the smell of hay in the snow, and the far owl*
> *Warning among the folds, and the frozen hold*
> *Flocked with the sheep white smoke of the farmhouse cowl*
> *In the river wended vales where the tale was told.*

at the moment of prayer for love:

> *Deliver him, he cried,*
> *By losing him all in love,*

Nature comes mystically alive from the past:

> *The nightingale*
> *Dust in the buried wood, flies on the grains of her*
> *wings . . .*
>
> *The wizened*
> *Stream with bells and baying water bounds. The dew rings*
> *On the gristed leaves and the long gone glistening*
> *Parish of snow. The carved mouths in the rock are*
> *wind swept strings.*

In this revivified natural world the she-bird, symbol of love,
rises, and the 'intricately' dead come miraculously to life in
delicate and precisely recorded images:

> *Look. And the dancers move*
> *On the departed, snow bushed green, wanton in moonlight*

As a dust of pigeons. Exulting, the grave hooved
Horses, centaur dead, turn and tread the drenched white
Paddocks in the farms of birds. The dead oak walks for love

The carved limbs in the rock
Leap, as to trumpets. Calligraphy of the old
Leaves is dancing.

In the moment of vision 'the time dying flesh' is overcome.

'In country sleep' is addressed to the poet's young daughter and in this 'tender and gentle exorcism of a child's fearful imagination'[23] he tells her not to fear the fictions of folk-tales or stories such as she may have been told before sleep:

Never and never, my girl riding far and near
In the land of the hearthstone tales, and spelled asleep,
Fear or believe that the wolf in a sheepwhite hood
Loping and bleating roughly and blithely shall leap . . .
To eat your heart in the house in the rosy wood.

Nor should she grow to fear sexuality:

no gooseherd or swine will turn
Into a homestall king or hamlet of fire
And prince of ice
To court the honeyed heart from your side . . .

for she is shielded in her 'country sleep': there is security in nature:

From the broomed witch's spume you are shielded by fern
And flower of country sleep and the greenwood keep.

20

The child's fear of sleep and dreams (fictions) should be forgotten since only death itself threatens, 'the stern Bell' that echoes and 'the Thief' who moves in time through the poem:

> *Never, my girl, until tolled to sleep by the stern*
> *Bell believe or fear that the rustic shade or spell*
> *Shall harrow and snow the blood . . .*

For the poet rejects the unreal ('moonshine') fears bred in legend or theology:

> *For who unmanningly haunts the mountain ravened eaves*
> *Or skulks in the dell moon but moonshine echoing*
> *clear . . .*

And it is death, not the agents of nature or sexuality that merits fear:

> *Fear most*
> *For ever of all not the wolf in his baaing hood*
> *Nor the tusked prince, in the ruttish farm, at the rind*
> *And mire of love, but the Thief as meek as the dew.*

The poet registers a complete faith in nature:

> *The country is holy: O bide in that country kind,*
> *Know the green good,*

With subtly evocative images drawn from the natural world, paradoxically tender and delicate in impact, Thomas suggests the unperceived but inevitable approach of death, the 'sly and sure' Thief who since the child's birth has been visitor:

> *Ever and ever he finds a way, as the snow falls,*
> *As the rain falls, hail on the fleece, as the vale mist rides*
> *Through the haygold stalls . . .*

21

Reading this evocation of the imperceptible growth of mortality even in the child one recalls Thomas's comment in the early letter:

> All thoughts and actions emanate from the body. Therefore the description of a thought — or action — however abstruse it may be — can be beaten home by bringing it onto a physical level.[24]

By a wholly characteristic paradox the poem concludes with the idea that in the cycle of nature death brings reimmersion into the natural world and what is lost (i.e. death steals or takes away) is only the belief that a heaven or hell follows. Paradoxically,[25] never need she grieve that this death (and reimmersion) will not happen, that she will be left forsaken and afraid, divorced from

> *The grains beyond age, the dark veins of her mother.*

'In the white giant's thigh' and 'Élegy' examine a man's soul as being born from nature and returning to it in death after a period when the soul lingers in memory. In the former poem, the longing of the women to love and conceive is expressed in terms of the creative energy of the natural world:

> *Through throats where many rivers meet, the curlews cry,.*
> *Under the conceiving moon, on the high chalk hill,*
> *And there this night I walk in the white giant's thigh*
> *Where barren as boulders women lie longing still*
>
> *To labour and love though they lay down long ago.*

The emotions and desires of the women are spoken of as remaining after death and even beyond memory:

> *Through throats where many rivers meet, the women pray,*

22

Pleading in the waded bay for the seed to flow
Though the names on their weed grown stones are rained
  away,

The poet builds a mythopoeic conception of their love as existing in nature: it is this 'evergreen' love that he seeks:

Teach me the love that is evergreen after the fall leaved
Grave, after Belovéd on the grass gulfed cross is scrubbed
Off by the sun and Daughters no longer grieved
Save by their long desires . . .

Similarly, but more personally and intimately, for it is a poem written (though unfinished when Dylan Thomas died) on his father's death, the poet suggests in 'Elegy' a continuing of love and renewed life in nature:

Oh, forever may
He lie lightly, at last, on the last, crossed
Hill, under the grass, in love, and there grow
Young among the long flocks, and never lie lost
Or still all the numberless days of his death . . .

There are echoes of the earlier 'the dark veins of her mother' ('A Refusal to Mourn . . . ') in the image that brings together the dead man's mother and nature as the final and universal mother:

Above all he longed for his mother's breast
Which was rest and dust, and in the kind ground
The darkest justice of death . . .

The poet images the very process of dying as a return to nature:

23

> *The rivers of the dead*
> *Veined his poor hand I held, and I saw*
> *Through his unseeing eyes to the roots of the sea.*

Clearly, then, in Dylan Thomas's poetry nature is neither a superficial pastoral escape nor a source of didactic sentiments: it is the vital life force in the universe. It may be the case, I suggest, that Thomas went beyond the simple division between human civilisation and nature, seeing man as in a state of being between the two, transiently linked with civilisation, but having come from and ultimately returning to 'the green good'. What cannot be doubted is that Thomas's profound appeal resides in his healing of man's sense of alienation from his roots in nature, an alienation acutely felt in the urban and technological society of today.

Notes
1. Fitzgibbon (ed.) *Selected Letters of Dylan Thomas,* London, 1966, p.47.
2. Forman (ed.), *The Letters of John Keats,* London, 1935, p.384.
3. 'I do not want to express only what other people have felt; I want to rip something away and show what they have never seen'- Dylan Thomas in a letter to Pamela Hansford Johnson in Sept. 1933, *Selected Letters of Dylan Thomas,* p.24.
4. Ibid., p.48.
5. Ibid.
6. Ibid.
7. 'Thomas seems to be saying that poetic vision comes not from mind but from heart and senses' - Tindall, *A Reader's Guide to Dylan Thomas,* London, 1962, p.161.
8. Cf. Blake's 'If the doors of perception were cleansed every-

thing would appear . . . infinite' (G.Keynes ed., *Blake: Poetry and Prose*, London, 1946, p.187.), and Dylan Thomas's statement, again in a letter, 'I am in the path of Blake, but so far behind him that only the wings of his heels are in sight' (*Selected Letters*, p.23).

9. Tindall, *A Reader's Guide to Dylan Thomas*, p.133.

10. Ibid.

11. W.E.Williams (ed.), *Wordsworth: A Selection*, London 1950, p.25.

12. H.N.Fairchild, *Religious Trends in English Poetry*, New York and London, 1968, Vol. VI, p.412.

13. W.E.Williams, op.cit., p.25.

14. Vernon Watkins, *Dylan Thomas: Letters to Vernon Watkins*, p.13.

15. *Selected Letters*, p.25.

16. H.N. Fairchild, op.cit., p.243.

17. C.Fitzgibbon, *Life of Dylan Thomas*, London, 1965, p.281.

18. Ibid., p.280.

19. Caitlin Thomas, *Leftover Life to kill*, London, 1957, p.36.

20. *Selected Letters*, p.24.

21. These were 'In country sleep', 'Over Sir John's hill', and 'In the white giant's thigh'.

22. Dylan Thomas, *Quite Early One Morning*, p.157.

23. Derek Stanford, *Dylan Thomas*, p.132.

24. Dylan Thomas, *Quite Early One Morning*, p.157.

25. Bearing in mind the complexity of theme and structure in this poem we may note Dylan Thomas's comment in another letter:
'I like things that are difficult to write and difficult to understand; I like 'redeeming the contraries' with secretive images' (*Selected Letters*, p.151).

SAUNDERS LEWIS:MORALITY PLAYWRIGHT

Pennar Davies

Despite occasional largely French-inspired aesthetistic sallies in his earlier years, sallies intended to disturb the complacency of those whom he once called the Tartuffes of Welsh literary criticism, Saunders Lewis is surely the most august moralist in twentieth century Welsh literature. As a moralist he is drastic, relentless, intransigent. His work - and I repeat that this must be said in spite of his own critical interest in literary forms, traditions, styles and uses of words - cannot be understood without recognising his ethical stringency; and so I want to approach him first of all through a play which axes through the anaesthetic moral sentimentality and even the indulgent humanitarianism of our age, one of his finest plays and less classifiable than most: *Amlyn ac Amig* (1940). He describes it as a 'comedy'. Apart from an ending for which the word 'happy' is insufficient and whose bliss is incredible to all but the faithful, the work trembles on the brink of tragedy.

Lewis has taken his medieval material and given it a new focus and a new dimension in two ways. It is Amlyn's crisis of conscience on which the play turns and not Amig's saintliness and sufferings; and the story is placed in the setting of the feast of the Nativity so that the slaying of Amlyn's sons inevitably connects with the Massacre of the Innocents (by

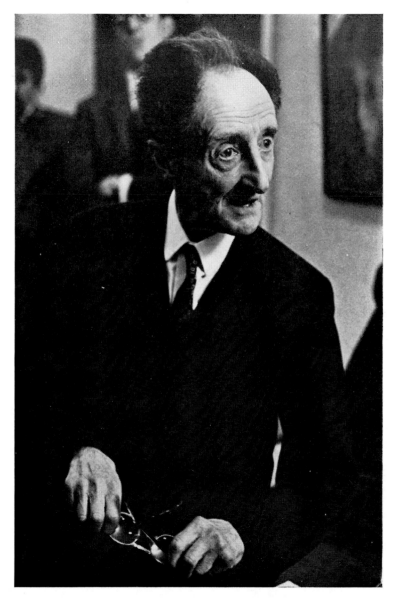

SAUNDERS LEWIS

teasing implication), and the agony of the hideous leper who is the peerless Friend of the soul that is in jeopardy touches upon the birth of the Lamb who is sent to die. These associations are both inevitable and excruciating. We are made to feel that all that comes to us is inexplicable apart from a cosmic transaction which is itself inexplicable. Lewis's art here is like that of the Four Branches of the Mabinogi in which the very incongruities have their own pregnant relevance to the wisdom that is imparted. Certainly we are compelled to acknowledge that human beings are one in the tangled tensions of their sufferings. See the cunning by which Saunders Lewis makes this explicit and calls us to compassion with a deliberate echoing of Virgil:

> *Yma hefyd mae dagrau am bethau dyn*
> *A throeon dynion yn cyffwrdd y galon ddynol.*

The tears of the play are the tears of all of us.

Yet the play alienates us as it possesses us. What are we to make of the outrageous demand that the children be sacrificed to cleanse the leper? We who live after Rousseau (who, we sometimes forget, managed to get rid of his children without actually killing them) cannot tolerate the unholy suggestion that the restoration of a leper, however far gone in rottenness, is worth the beheading of a brace of youngsters still carefree in their relative innocence and simplicity. This kind of thing was often done in the old days, but we have learnt - quite properly - to condemn Jephthah's vow and to praise the Abraham who took his son home safe rather than the Abraham who took his son out to die. I have no doubt that we are right. I confess that I could not have used this plot without changing it. But my impression is that Saunders Lewis presents this extravagance of rigorism with relish. And yet it is not that he would add to Tertullian's *quia impossibile* his own *quia indignissimum*.

His sole purpose is to compel us to face the utterly dis-
concerting questions: Why are we here? Is it only that we
may enjoy power, plenty and pleasure for a brief season? Or
is it that our souls should be saved alive? The primary
interest of the blest yet nightmarish story for Saunders Lewis
is not what may happen to the body of Amig or to the bodies
of the children but what may happen to Amlyn's agonizing
soul. It is his self-love that has to be slain, the self-love that
taints even his love for his children. Saunders Lewis is not
content with the pagan decencies, however engaging. He
sees us all as in need of the spiritual operation that only the
white-clad surgeon Christ can perform, if I may borrow the
imagery of one of Gwenallt's finest poems. It is interesting
that an exquisite play of soul-making should have a place of
central significance in the work of an artist who once re-
buked Tegla Davies's fatal habit of seeking to convert his
characters.

It is of importance to understand that Amlyn's conversion
is not completed by the act of self-denial presented in so
excoriating a way. For he does it grudgingly, loathing
himself and God: 'heaven is not a giver but a bargainer'. He
still has to know God the giver - in the restoration of his
friend and his family. The whole of the old story is as rel-
evant to Saunders Lewis's purpose as is the framework of the
Book of Job (casually dismissed by some critics who should
know better) to the dramatic portrayal of another soul in
crisis.

I have suggested that Saunders Lewis's other plays are
more classifiable. They can be divided roughly into two
kinds (according to their thematic interests), plays concerned with the crisis of the Welsh people and of Christian
civilisation in our own age and plays concerned with sexual
love, self-fulfillment and society. The two domains overlap
and there is sometimes cross-fertilisation of ideas, but they
can be distinguished. Let us turn to the first of the two.

We are conscious as we read *Buchedd Garmon* (The Life of Garmon) (1937), a play of uncommon power and nobility, that we are contemplating the twentieth century through the veil of the fifth. A Christian civilisation is being threatened by the destructiveness of marauding barbarians. A pivotal area in the struggle is the land of the Romano-Britons or early Welsh who led by Emrys are seeking to defend their inheritance against the Saxon heathens; but here the military enterprise is imperilled by the ideological clash between the faith of Christendom championed by Garmon and the individualism and humanism of the brilliant but perverse heresiarch Pelagius. Lewis handles the history in a somewhat cavalier fashion, not endeavouring overmuch to avoid anachronisms or to eliminate hagiography; and his treatment of Pelagius is more generous than just. The masterly pageant-play is really a burningly eloquent tract for our times, and the Wales and the world of 1936 are meant to shine through: political desperation, economic misery, spiritual need. There is speechifying enough, as grand as Saunders Lewis himself in the dock; and there are shouts, cries and earthy invective. And there is symbolism: the beggarwoman and the blind child represent Wales and the deliverers are - like the stripling Nationalist movement - 'a despised little party that would save their country'. There is no inward conflict in the hero, and so the play lacks the dramatic tension of *Amlyn ac Amig* or Eliot's *Murder in the Cathedral*, (the latter inviting an inevitable comparison). On the other hand, I find it difficult to think of a more refulgent dramatic manifesto: if we had a latter-day Handel in our midst he could not find better material for a rival to *Judas Maccabaeus*.

Now we leap across some twenty years into post-war Europe in *Gymerwch chi Sigaret?* (Will you take a Cigarette?), (1956), a 'well-made play', whether we like it or not - and Lewis does not seem to have succumbed at all to the modern straggling episodic fashion - and a topical one dramatizing the conflict between Christian civilisation (Catholic, if you will: we do not expect Saunders Lewis to draw too rigid a line of demarcation between the two words) and the threat of Communism in an East European country. We are not left in doubt as to which side is favoured by God and the author, but the charge of anti-communist propaganda brought against the play is sheerly imperceptive. If we find sacrificial martyrdom (in the person of Iris) and practical devotion (in the person of Phugas) on the Christian side only, it is because Lewis is a Christian and not because he is writing an anti-communist play. The ingenious trick on which the plot turns - the substitution of the rosary for the bullet in the cigarette-case which is a disguised revolver - is a little embarrassing, rather more so than the ringing of the telephone in *Saer Doliau,* Gwenlyn Parry's equally accomplished essay in a different kind of dramatic idiom. I gladly acknowledge in both cases the stunning theatric effectiveness and reverberating symbolism of the device; but in *Gymerwch chi Sigaret?* it has the consequence of diverting attention from the real action of the play, the action that takes place in the soul of Marc. For this, like *Amlyn ac Amig,* is the drama of a soul in crisis; and Iris corresponds to Amig in the sense that both of them as they suffer are the agents of a providential strategy that they are far from fully understanding. Whether we are meant to believe (as I would willingly do) that in their suffering they participate in an ongoing *Heilsgeschichte* must be left to each of us to decide; and this may have been the author's intention.

It might well be argued that *Brad* (Treachery; Betrayal), (1958), is Lewis's supreme masterpiece of dramatic construction in the tradition of the 'well-made play'. And it illustrates and yet, in another sense, runs counter to what I have already said about his ethical rigorism. We are introduced to a complex of relationships and their accompanying loyalties X-rayed by the excitement and horror of the abortive July 1944 plot against Hitler as the relentless events involved a number of persons highly placed in the German army in France. We see in them conflicts of commitment, and we watch them being sickeningly tempted to betray one or another of their loyalties - loyalties to Europe, to Germany, to comrades, to military superiors, to humanity, to a benefactor, to a lover, to an ideal of chastity without which human love must suffer degradation. Within the limits imposed by the situation presented this miracle of the dramatic art brings to us a well-nigh exhaustive treatment of the ethical issues. It is rigorist in the sense that it confronts us with these issues and will not let us escape; but it is unlike most of Lewis's work in that here he does not overtly proclaim his own judgement but for the most part leaves us to make ours. Knowing Saunders Lewis we may feel sure that we are in the end meant to spurn von Kluge's reluctance to venture and meant too to sympathize with those who are concerned for the common heritage of western Europe. But he seems pledged not to intrude his own view as he allows the characters to explain and excuse themselves, even Albrecht, the Nazi. At the end we share the measureless grief of Else's vain surrender of her chastity to Albrecht in order to save her lover. In an age in which chastity is derided rather than revered this particular issue may seem a throw-back to the last century; but if we accept its relevance we are not spared by any sentimentality the agony of the moral dilemma.

This particular motif, the willingness of a chaste woman to yield her body in order that a good end may be served, becomes even more central in two other plays that speak to the condition of a community in crisis, *Esther* (1960) and *Cymru Fydd* (The Wales that shall be) (1967). Esther acts as she does in order to deliver the Jews from extermination.

Haman's wicked ambition has a double reference - to
Hitler's 'final solution' of the Jewish problem and to the
slower and slyer method of genocide used by the English
state against the Welsh nation for, by this time, more than
four centuries. It would be interesting to trace the inter-
twining of the two strands; but there is an even wider application of the theme of the play, for Haman also serves to point
the moral that the assumption of absolute power by a tyrant
or an oligarchy is the ultimate blasphemy, the very usurp-
ation of God's own power. Haman coolly defines politics as
'man seeking to become God'. The politician's paradise, he
says, is to make death an instrument in his hands. And so, as
he sentences the whole Jewish nation to death, he exults at
the thought that he is for them none other than God.
Haman's reflections are monstrous enough to justify a comparison with some of Dostoyevsky's creations. He sees the
day coming when a man, some head of state or commander
of armed forces, will be able to take a ball of fire in his hands
and fling it so as to destroy all humanity, a   universal assass-
ination which will be the end of the world - the inevitable
end, for what man could resist the temptation of the experience of being God? Here we have a variant of the Antichrist
concept on which Saunders Lewis had already written his
great sonnet 'Y Dewis' which confronts the final all-
conquering Ozymandias of human history with the
gibbeted Victim whom all his cunning and violence cannot
avail to exorcise. A further comment (which Lewis's sense of
dramatic unity and fitness would not allow him to make in
Esther) is provided by another poem, the equally overwhelming 'I'r Lleidr Da' in which we see the Victim holding
his royal court on the cross.

Cymru Fydd, I take it, is more of a warning than a pre-
diction. Saunders Lewis always resolutely exposes the
foulest in our national psyche. As president of the Welsh
Language Society he knows something about the cheerful

enthusiasm with which some of our young people collect sentences of imprisonment for defying the laws which insult and degrade their language. But, nauseated, I believe, by an incident in which some protesters of this goodly type were manhandled by ruffians with the connivance or encouragement of the police, he chooses in this play to present under its provocative title a young man who has become a moral nihilist and who is not only an unrepentant delinquent of the ignoblest sort but is willing to deceive and exploit the girl who loves him before he seeks an escape through suicide. He makes the young man - no doubt as a salutary admonition to present-day Welsh Christianity - a son of the manse, perhaps overlooking the notable contribution that the manse has made to the Welsh Language Society. But of course - and here we have an aspect of the play strangely missed by some of its hostile critics - he places with the young man under the same jabbing title of *Cymru Fydd* the girl Bet, a daughter of the vicarage and as important at least as Dewi in the plot and the thesis of the work. For as against his nihilism she ventures in faith, the faith which is itself a venture. She represents Pascal's wager as understood by Saunders Lewis; and it appears that the name 'Bet' is intended to have this significance. Pascal's famous persuasive - that wisdom takes a bet that God exists - has been interpreted and denounced as a miserable prudential argument; but as Lewis handles it, it partakes of the nature of the passionate 'leap' of Jacobi and Kierkegaard - an almost existential wagering on the truth that demands our all. In her *particular* gamble on the postulate of Dewi's ultimate remediability she loses heavily, but this does not invalidate the immeasurably more momentous venture of taking a bet on the ultimate quiddity of existence. It is Bet who redeems the play from melodrama.

Europe and the world, Wales and Christendom, crisis and choice for soul and society - it is these that dominate the plays at which we have glanced so far. And there are other pieces, lighter in manner and yet scathing and sardonic enough, like *Eisteddfod Bodran* and *Problemau Prifysgol,* which touch upon these matters in the comic context of the oddities of Welsh life and Welsh institutions such as the Eisteddfod and the University (usually so much more solemnly discussed). These satirical works deserve to be more thoroughly examined than they have been, but I am now beckoned by the other class of plays and must turn to them, the plays of sexual entanglements and the demands of society upon the individual.

Lewis's earliest literary interest (apart from literary history and scholarship) was the psychology of the lover and the artist. During the twenties he published his English playlet *The Eve of Saint John* (1921), linguistically an attempt to convey through English the rhythms and idioms of Welsh, his first Welsh play *Gwaed yr Uchelwyr* ('Blood of the Nobles' might be a better rendering than many) (1922), his critical-historical study *A School of Welsh Augustans* (1924) and some truly epoch-making critical contributions including his essay on Dafydd Nanmor (1925), his amazing *Williams Pantycelyn* (1927) and scarcely less original *Ceiriog* (1929); and he rounded off the decade's output in 1930 with his clinical treatment of love and marriage in the short novel *Monica.* Psychological and sociological interests are evident in the critical work as well as in the two plays and the novel. The treatment of love, sexual love between the male and the female of the species, is from the very beginning untainted by the romantic idealisation of it which has been dominant in European literature until comparatively recent times. I think that it will be found undeniable - though it is still unrecognised in nearly all popular and most of the learned studies of the subject - that the Welsh stimulus to this idealisation in the Middle Ages was paramount for good or ill. The truth is that it has been for both good and ill. On the one hand, 'romantic love' has been a hallowing of Christian monogamy and an expression of the liberty, equality and mutual responsibility of the sexes; on the other, it has, in its sentimentalised and vulgarised forms, been perhaps the most vicious spiritual drug that has corrupted human relationships from the days of the *amour courtois* until now, and the commercial exploitation of it in brash or blasé novels, plays and films remains a formidable barrier between the human mind and reality. Saunders Lewis's view of it from the beginning - as shown deliciously in *The Eve of Saint John* - has been miraculously free from illusion. He sees it, in its imaginative expression, as sexual fantasy springing from the cravings of the flesh. 'Don't I see him plain before me *the moment I shut my eyes?*' says Megan to the rejected Harri. 'A strong man with a beard would blunt the edge of a new scythe, and great muscles to his chest, and it rough and hairy.' On the Eve of Saint John Megan sells her soul to the devil in order to satisfy her carnal desire. Even when she realises what she has done she still rejects a marriage that would not bring her what she wants; and the rejection means forfeiting solid comforts and status. Hers is the rebellious *eros* that threatens the structure of society.

The contrast between Megan and Luned, the heroine of *Gwaed yr Uchelwyr,* could not be sharper; it is as if it has been done by design. And yet, curiously, the two have in common a rejection of marriage and a resistence to the claims and pressures of society. The story of Saunders Lewis's first play in Welsh makes use of some of the stock-in-trade of the Welsh drama of that period. We have the Squire who represents oppressive landlordism; a farmer's daughter who loves and is loved by the Squire's son; the burning of the hayricks of the landlord's steward; the endangering of the life of the farmer and of the persistence of the family tradition in the farm - all pointing to the sweetmeat that

Saunders Lewis withholds from his audience, the solution
of all the problems by the marriage of the young people. Out
of these too promising ingredients, Lewis has fashioned the
oddest concoction in the history of Welsh drama. The Isallt
family is really of a superior breed to that of the Squire, for
they are descended from the old Welsh princes. (So, it has
been calculated, do most of the Welsh, though the blood of
the *uchelwyr* is somewhat diluted in them.) Luned's mother
urges her to marry Arthur, the Squire's son, in order to save
her father's life and their Isallt heritage. She is tempted to do
this, though it is hateful to her to enter marriage under the
compulsion of circumstance. When it is learned that her
father's life is not in danger but that they must leave Isallt
she thanks God for her release from temptation and feels
that she is now free to make her own choice. Her choice is
not to marry. Since this means the loss of Isallt, she chooses
also exile and virginity. Thus the play bids defiance to the
conventions of romance and enthrones the austerity of the
ascetic tradition: it is a capital example of Lewis's ethical
rigorism and it is at the same time of a piece with the long
story of man's strivings after the ardours of renunciation and
abstinence. Yet all this is given us in a by no means wholly
Christian context; and Luned's exercise in radical selfdenial
involves an impoverishment of the inheritance of her
people. Luned's moral extremism is in a sense as anti-social
as Megan's sensual self-indulgence. Both heroines are unrepentant prodigals; but the far country of the one is the nun-
nery while the other is well set for the brothel. The centrality
given in *Gwaed yr Uchelwyr* to choosing and to the freedom
to choose links the play — perhaps not so strangely as you
might suppose - with modern existentialist literature. It is
not unconnected with Lewis's interpretation of Pascal's
wager in the much later *Cymru Fydd*.

It is not surprising that writing or having written these
two early plays he found himself attracted by the story of

Blodeuwedd in the fourth of the Four Branches of the *Mabinogi,* and an incomplete attempt to write a play on her found a hopeful welcome on the pages of the *Llenor* in 1923 and 1925. Poetic drama has its own problems and the completed *Blodeuwedd* was not written until 1947 and was published in the following year. It was in the novel *Monica* that Lewis essayed to demolish the 'romantic love' which he felt to be rooted in the flesh and, as he says in his *Williams Pantycelyn,* to set up an absolute claim and to offer an all-sufficient paradise. *Monica* is an anti-love story, the most powerful anti-aphrodisiac I have encountered in literature, a second *Madame Bovary* all the more concentrated for being in miniature.

After his conversion to Roman Catholicism we have more than one piece of poetic evidence of the attraction exercised upon him by the figure of Mary Magdalen. I have been hoping against hope for a full-length stage-play by him on the old legend (of which he has made use) that the disciple John in order to follow Christ repudiated the Magdalen's love for him and that she, in consequence, drifted despairingly into a life of fornication. The story is tailor-made for the author of *Gwaed yr Uchelwyr, Monica* and *Blodeuwedd.* I suspect that he has been held back by a certain reticence, devotionally or theologically motivated, from handling too intimately a theme which touches so closely the earthly life of Jesus: I seem to remember a review by Lewis of *Yr Ogof,* the novel by T. Rowland Hughes set against the background of events centring in the Passion, a review which expressed a certain unease about any attempt in literature to show the historical Jesus among the tensions of his times.

It is in *Blodeuwedd* that Saunders Lewis has given us the tragedy of romantic love in the sense in which he under-ands the term. It is a surely undeniable masterpiece of poetic drama. Its uncanny achievement is to give to this essentially

37

carnal love, with all its deceitfulness and destructiveness, a rare magnificence which is different from any kind of splendour which may be appropriate in a treatment of romantic love differently understood. That the author of the squalid *Monica* should be also the author of the resplendent *Blodeuwedd* and should present in them the same values is a most rewarding problem in aesthetics. It is not - not at any rate as is commonly meant by the terms - the difference between realism and romance. It is rather that in *Blodeuwedd* Lewis transposes the theme to a new key and so brings off a triumph comparable with Shakespeare's *Anthony and Cleopatra* - with the difference that while Shakespeare's play has a kind of oriental opulence, Lewis's gives us the flavour of Cymric mythology with its eerie interplay between two worlds and between sense and symbol. Blodeuwedd is a creature of nature and of art, and in making the fullest use of this duality Saunders Lewis is faithfully interpreting the amazing work which is his source; but of course he brings out the contrast in the dialogue and is clearly applying it to his doctrine of the baseness of romantic love. The love that is here condemned is compounded of the natural and the unnatural, of lust and fantasy, of blazing desire and cold illusion. We hear of Blodeuwedd's 'heart of ice' and of 'the fury of her kiss'. She would be loved 'for her own sake'; she is not bound to family or kindred. She cares nothing for constancy: it is for lust alone that she lives. Her beauty is the callous beauty of the moon, and under Gwydion's retributive curse she is exiled 'to the darkness with the owls', to the modes of 'the moon and the hollow tree'. Her adulterous lover Gronw Pebr accepts the suzereignty of her loveliness and enthrones her imperious will in his life. Rhagnell the maid is likewise subject to her. Both of them find release only in death. The condemnation of Blodeuwedd, of the ruthlessness and the wiles of unchaste passion rioting in the flesh and in the imagination, could

not be more severe; and yet Saunders Lewis, possessed by the
enchantment of the old tale and also, perhaps, mellowing
somewhat in spite of himself, is compelled to acknowledge
her beauty. In *Monica* the beauty of romantic love had not
been even grudgingly allowed.

If it is right to speak of a mellowing process, it is certainly
further advanced in *Siwan* (broadcast in 1954), a 'creative
poem', the author assures us disarmingly, 'not the work of a
historian'. Nevertheless, there is no denying the dexterity
with which he handles history in this closely knit,
astonishingly devised treatment of the adultery of the thirty-
five year old Siwan (Joan), daughter of King John of
England and wife of the fifty-seven year old Llywelyn the
Great - the ages of the *dramatis personae* are supplied in the
list preceding the play in its published form - with the
twenty-five year old Gwilym Brewys (William de Braose).
But our concern is with the love passages. Saunders Lewis
ought to be and is on the side of Llywelyn, but by or against
his will he has given the tempted Siwan and Gwilym an irresistible attraction for each other and for the audience. The
young father of four daughters, Gwilym is nevertheless a
bonny Tristram, and although fifteen years have passed
since Siwan bestowed an Iseult kiss on the ten year old lad
she is more than equal to the destiny thus laid upon him,
and the taste of her love kindles in him an inescapable desire
in which pain and delight are mingled. He says that he wor-
ships her, and for Lewis this has always been the language of
romantic love. In the dialogue Marie de France and the
troubadours, Hywel ab Owain and Francis of Assisi are
invoked to lend enchantment to the sweet adultery; even the
silken songs of the Arabs are not forgotten. There is for the
time more indulgence if less pity in this first act of the play
than there is in Dante's tender etching of Paolo and
Francesca. Even in the second, in which Gwilym Brewys is
hanged, the glamour does not evaporate. 'There is a power',

says Siwan, 'like a supernatural power in the impact; it is as well for men that love is rare in the world.' Whether this is meant to be true or to be regarded as a delusion of the flesh, we are not told; but we are emphatically worlds away from the ruthless exposé of romantic love in *The Eve of Saint John, Monica,* or even *Blodeuwedd.* But that Saunders Lewis by this time is more than willing to tolerate something akin to romantic love becomes abundantly clear in the third act, in which Llywelyn himself confesses that he is not immune: he says that when Siwan came to him a virgin like a fresh silver birch his heart gave a sudden turn as if he had seen the Grail - and this is extravagant language even for high romance. When a little later Llywelyn says that all that he has done for their son Dafydd has been an expression of his love for her, a temple raised in her honour, when he speaks of it even as his 'worship' for her, we are entitled to conclude that Lewis is now prepared to accord a place to a 'romantic' kind of sexual passion within the discipline of family, community and faith, within the 'purgatory' which, as Llywelyn says, is the best blessing that marriage can bring.

Lewis's exquisite 'historical romance' *Merch Gwern Hywel (1964)* is, if anything, mellower, I must content myself with the briefest comment on this delicately done *Novelle.* Mrs. Jones, Gwern Hywel, condemns roundly (echoing, you feel, the early Saunders Lewis) that 'falling in love' which is nothing but 'coupling lust disguising itself as religion'; but by implication her philosophy of marriage is repudiated by the whole tone of the narrative as reducing it to the level of an economic bargain between families. There is a third view, the Methodist view expounded by John Roberts and put daringly into practice by the eloping lovers, Sarah Jones and William Roberts - godly marriage within the faith, marriage based on mutual esteem and a shared devotion, on the deep regard of the pledged persons for each other. The Calvinistic Methodists of Wales, by forbidding marriage outside the *soseiad*, had sanctioned and promoted this conception of an evangelical love not unrelated to romantic love. John Roberts has to concede, somewhat ruefully: 'That is a romantic falling in love, and it is our rules that have bred it'. It has taken Saunders Lewis a long time to envisage a sort of romantic love that is distinguishable from Monica's, but his progress towards it has given us some of the century's masterworks of imaginative literature.

THE MYTHOLOGY OF THE MINING VALLEYS

Glyn Tegai Hughes

The army of stage Welshmen, coal-dust on the boots and *Cwm Rhondda* on the lips, paraded rather late. The mining novels may be set in the late nineteenth century, but they were not written for fifty years or more. A culture tends to create its myths from the past. A community glorifies itself when it is breaking up.

The conscious creation of myth is rare and difficult; the early German Romantic writers attempted it and, to a large measure, fell over into allegory. The development of existing patterns of myth is, of course, the norm until the later eighteenth century and, even then, Classical Antiquity and Biblical themes tend to be replaced by equally antique systems drawn from the national past—Germanic or Celtic often enough. Geographical displacement makes it possible for Tahiti or America to acquire the status of myth for the eighteenth century European mind; but the emergence of myth from the near past is a fairly recent development. The model, perhaps, is the opening up of the American West. More conscious recent formulations might be the Long March for the Chinese and the Life of Lenin for the Russians. Their special feature is that they are supported by a massive framework of propagandist education by the state. So, to some extent, was the myth of the British Empire, now so comprehensively debunked, even if somewhat unjustly and with displeasing relish.

The time-scale of myth-making is, however, an uncertain one. Distancing by time, or by geography, has hitherto seemed to be necessary, on the principle of no man being a hero to his valet. Yet the contemporary media, which ought, because of their direct reporting to be restricting mythopeic tendencies, have clearly not done this with Che Guevara. Perhaps it is enough that he is dead.

The myth enables men to identify. We are able to ally ourselves with something greater than ourselves, with some eternal state of being, with powers moving in or above history. A prime example showing this at one remove is Joyce's use in *Ulysses* of existing Homeric, Biblical and Shakespearean myths to suggest both recurring human patterns and contemporary impoverishment. The point was made in a famous passage by Joseph Warren Beach: 'Those poor soused Dubliners stand at the bar and discuss the topics of the day, the death of Paddy Dignam, the foot-and-mouth disease, the Irish language, and their drinks. And somewhere out of Eternity there comes a weird light to throw their shadows on some apocalyptic screen: monstrous swollen, misshapen shadows as of mythical heroes, carrying out in pantomime on some prodigious scale the ideal implications of their petty words.' And this for a nation already gorged with history, drenched with its own myths, from Cuchulain to the Easter Rising.

And what has Wales to offer, faced with all this? I argue elsewhere that we created in the nineteenth century an identification of Wales and the Holy Land that was itself myth-making. But this had certainly faded away long before Idris Davies wrote his 'London Welsh' in the 1940s:

We have scratched our names in the London dust,
Sung sometimes like the Jews of Babylon

> *Under the dusty trees of Hyde Park Corner,*
> *Almost believing in a Jesus of Cardigan*
> *Or a Moses on the mountains of Merioneth.*

What the novel of the 1930s shows is the gradual flowering of a new myth, the idealised picture of the South Wales valleys.

It is surprising how little, comparatively, was written in English or Welsh about the mining valleys before the 1930s. It may, therefore, be worth looking at one of the first extended accounts of the daily life of the Welsh miner, published anonymously in the quarterly *Yr Adolygydd* in 1853.[2] The year, we may remind ourselves, was one of comparative quiet in the industry; wage rates were, by the low standards of the collier's earnings, not unduly depressed and attempts at unionism were no more than sporadic. The great growth in momentum was just underway: in 1800 the South Wales pits had employed some 12,000 men; by 1853 there were something over 30,000; by 1883, 80,000; and by 1903, 160,000.[3]

The anonymous contributor begins, like Jack Jones in *Bidden to the Feast,* with the child miner. He may start work, at 6d a day, when he is eight or ten, but often younger, and he will be employed opening and closing the air doors. Though not hard work it is unhealthy and dangerous, with an equal danger to morals through exposure to the oaths of the hauliers. He may also start with his father on the face and this is certainly safer, in spite of the continual dangers to which all miners are exposed. The child will be awakened between three and four in the morning and will often not see the sun at all; his connexion with nature is severed.

This, perhaps the most strongly emphasised of all features of the miner's life, is supported by a good deal of fine writing: 'Thus the miner spends many days without ever seeing the monarch of the day and his bright rays, and hearing no sound but subterranean tones. Often, night and morning, he sees only the light of moon and stars, and in the long days of Summer he is awakened at dawning, when the sun rises above the Eastern mountains and begins to pour forth its light and to show nature in its beauty and verdure; the flowers opening, the meadows dappled with primroses, and the clover-covered fields spreading their scent . . . ' and continuing with the woods, the birds, the breeze from the hills. All this contrasted with the candlelight, the evil air, the sulphurous fumes of explosions and the smoke of the powder. (There is an interesting possible comparison here with earlier attitudes to mining—generally, of course, not of coal— where emphasis is laid on the contact offered with entirely new aspects of nature underground.)

The customs of the miners are, in part, good; but there are also many depraved aspects. They are, to start with the good, usually hard-working and they wash at the end of each day. In summer one often finds three to six of them sitting outdoors discussing their work or the events of the day. 'Generally each one will be sitting on his haunches, his shirt open at the collar and with no kerchief round his neck, and all with a pipe between their teeth.' Little work is done at the beginning of the month and almost none on Monday. The drinkers spend these days in the taverns, and the talk is of fighting, the oppression of the employers or the deceitfulness of the weighers, of races, of the quality of the beer, or the character of the landlord. But recently also of politics, the attractions of emigration and news from America; and sometimes even of religion, especially by way of comment on preachers and ministers. The writer wishes that the men could be paid weekly; he does not want them to work harder, but more regularly. Again, he is not opposed to union for good, but the unions of masters and men are founded to fight one another, and there must be a better way than this. He ends with an appeal for more understanding, and for a clearer recognition of our debt to the miner.

Now all this is pitched at a cool enough level and much of the material could be paralleled in Blue Books such as the reports of the *Children's Employment Commission,* 1842 and *The State of the Population in Mining Districts,* 1846 and 1850. Working conditions are described in some detail; living conditions scarcely at all. Apart from horror at the deprivation of light, all is in a fairly low key. The community figures only by implication and certainly less so than in accounts of village life. The sense of valley life as being something special has not yet begun.

Until his death in February, 1852, *Yr Adolygydd* had as one of its editors Evan Jones, Ieuan Gwynedd; and a poem he wrote three days before his death is the one authentic horrified look at the miner's life that we get in the nineteenth century. 'The Song of the Miner' ('Can y Glowr'), with its incessant refrain 'glo, glo, glo!', sets the unthinking demand for coal against the realities of a miner's life: rock-fall, foul air, water, gas. The coal burns the miner alive and blows him to pieces ('Nes llosgi'n fyw y glowr tlawd, A'i chwythu'n ddarnau mân'); it is mingled with his flesh and his blood ('Ac er mai cymysgedig yw A dynol waed a chnawd'); in cutting it he digs his own grave ('Am wneud i mi, wrth dori glo, Ar unwaith dori'm bedd!')

For the rest, the whole of the second half of the nineteenth century has little, almost nothing indeed, about the life of the miner or the mining valleys in either Welsh or English. There are certainly a good number of Welsh ballads[4] with such titles as 'Galargerdd am y Ddamwain Ofnadwy ar y 15ed o Orffennaf, 1856 yng Ngwaith Glo Insole and Co., yn y Cymer, gerllaw Pont-y-pridd' ('Elegy on the dreadful calamity at Insole and Co.'s pit at Cymer near Pontypridd on the 15th of July, 1856'). These ballads frequently illuminate social conditions but they tend to do so indirectly; they are not generally about a community, but about particular noteworthy events, especially of a criminal or a calamitous kind. They do not elevate circumstances, but encapsulate it to titillate an unlettered audience.

There are occasional poems by a good number of more conscious artists (Ceiriog, Ben Bowen, Ossian Gwent, Watcyn Wyn, and—marginally—Islwyn). Some sketches by T. Mardy Rees[5] are no more than vehicles for some lamentably unfunny anecdotes; but they do show an attempt at reproducing dialect and at establishing not wholly unrealistic comic characters in a mining community. A number of stories, for instance, centre around 'Y Bachan Main' ('The thin fellow').

But there is one other work that uses the mining context to significant effect, the one-act play *Ble Mà Fa?* by D.T.Davies.[6] Gitto has been killed in a roof fall and, as he was not a chapel member, as he did not believe, his widow is gravely distressed by the theological consequences: where is he now? All that she has learnt from childhood leads her to a cruel but inescapable conclusion; but one that is not verified by her knowledge of Gitto. The tragedy is in the conflict of belief and experience. The starkness of the setting in the mining context, and the quality of the dialogue with its modified dialect, succeed in snatching nobility out of sentiment and suggesting some degree of universality. It is the nearest approach to a Welsh *Riders to the Sea*.

If the mining background is shadowy in Welsh writing before the First War, is it any more distinct in English? As a literary setting its most lavish use is certainly in the novels and stories of Joseph Keating (1871-1934). These are stiff and stagy in plot and characterisation, but present a fairly knowledgeable picture of the physical conditions of mining; in the course of a somewhat drifting life Keating had spent six years in the mines. They also show an awareness of shifting social patterns in the valleys and, even more acutely, a vivid sense of loss as they saw the green hillsides of Mountain Ash succumb to the final assault of coal, with 'the old pastoral life of our village being slowly changed into a hideous industrial existence'.[7] There are points of considerable interest in Keating's work, such as the concern with Welsh tradition and mythology, as in the digressions on the Mabinogion in *Maurice* (1905). A good number of later motifs – chapels, explosions, rescues, the bosses, the English influence, the un-greening of the valleys – are to be found in his works; and yet they remain cold fictions, novelistic graft-ings onto reality.

An attempt to grapple with the religious and political changes of a mining town (Aberpandy — Tonypandy) was made by J.O.Francis in 1912 in his four-act play, *Change*, published in Aberystwyth in the following year as the second of the Welsh Plays series of which *Ble Mà Fa?* was the first. Snatches of the dialogue will convey the atmosphere: 'I remember Aberpandy before ever the Powell-Griffiths sank the first pit, and the sheep of Pandy Farm were grazing quietly where the Bryndu Pit is now.' 'Ah yes! It isn't like it was when we'd have to bring the benches out of the vestry on a Sunday night.' 'He (the father) belongs to the old valley. At heart he's of the agricultural class — slow, stolid, and con-servative. You, Lewis (the revolutionary son), you're of a different kind altogether — you've grown up in modern industry, with no roots in the soil. That's why you're a rebel.' Faults of construction, undistinguished dialogue and rather contrived situations limit its effectiveness as a play; but as a mirror of the confusions of its time and the shifting allegiances of the valleys it is a useful if naive social docu-ment.

After the First World War there is little literature about the valleys until the Depression gathered momentum in the 1930's. Rhys Davies, it is true, used the mining background in stories and novels before 1930. *A Bed of Feathers* (1929) or *Rings on her Fingers* (1930) are set squarely enough in a mining community and yet the view is in some way detached, wary, hostile. *Rings on her Fingers* opens like this: 'The home was in a gathering of better-class houses that cluster, dingy and pretentious, in a little west-end of the Valley, dusty stone villas occupied by retired tradesmen, chapel ministers, engineers of the colliery, bank cashiers and others: a quiet community.' The oppressive forces of capital, Nonconformity, respectability are buttressed by what he later calls (*The Story of Wales*,1943, p.33) 'the ungainly ugliness of the coalfields, with their crowded grimy rows of little dwellings'. In the same paragraph he speaks of the change from 'the quality of calm constancy in the nature of (the countryman's) being' to the insecurity of the miner's lot with falling wages, strikes, lock-outs, and all the economic ills attendant on the industry, and with the dangers of coal-mining providing 'a sense of disaster forever lurking in the air'.

Rhys Davies[8] later addresses himself more directly to the social and political problems of insecurity and rebellion, notably in *A Time to Laugh* (written in 1937 and published in 1942), *Jubilee Blues* (1938) and *Tomorrow to Fresh Woods* (1941). Yet he is interested in the individuals rather than in the community, in the analysis of character (and sometimes, indeed, the manipulation of stereotypes) rather than the creation of myth. In his autobiographical *Print of a Hare's Foot*, (London, 1969) he registers the clichés lovingly: 'The place (Clydach) gave birth to a champion boxer, preached magnificent sermons and, inescapably, it sang. I knew only one of its three hard-worked midwives— well-informed Mrs. Bowen Small Bag, rightly a great gossip, who brought me expertly into the world while the new century was still taking stock of its advantages, and to whom I never thought of sending a bunch of flowers until too late. Like all the Rhondda, Clydach trumpeted an affirmation of the constructive urge in man.' In the novels, however, the trumpets are muted. Or, at any rate, they are very much single instruments. The mining valleys are the backcloth for the struggle between Lawrentian passion and petrification, or between materialism and artistic ideals.

By the 1930s the problems of the valleys had acquired a spectral intensity of their own. Beyond Tonypandy and the General Strike there had come the grinding horror of mass-unemployment. From the early months of 1929 to early 1931 it more than doubled, and from about September 1931 to the later months of 1933 it held an even higher level. By the summer of 1935 it was back to the level of the summer of 1930. At its peak, in the summer of 1932, the unemployment rate in Wales was over 38 per cent.

Dole-queues, hunger marches, soup kitchens and cast-off clothing, the parcels from London for doling out in the Brynmawrs and Nantyglos. Men working in water up to their thighs but lucky, others in the same street having been out of work for seven years—on the margins of recollection statistics are, for some of us, supported by life. And, for all of us, the emigration of some 400,000 people from South Wales between 1920 and 1939 is a shaping fact of our national life.

The Depression all but killed the mining communities; it drained them of their men and sapped the will of those who remained. The valleys had not only ceased to be green, they were in full decay.

One reaction to such a state is the wholly political one we see in the novels of Lewis Jones, *Cwmardy* (1937) and *We Live* (1939). The novels cover a period from the end of the nineteenth century to the late 1930s and are frankly documents of class-warfare. Len's last letter to Mary from Spain ends: 'Give my love to all the comrades at home. Throw your whole weight into the Party. Tell mam and dad not to worry about me. Sleep happy in the knowledge that our lives have been class lives, and our love something buried so deep in the Party that it can never die.' James Hanley, reviewing

Cwmardy in the *London Mercury* of August 1937, admits
that the novel has no pretensions to being a piece of literature: 'But I cannot see that the canons of literary criticism
should be applied to books like these. They serve their
purpose, which is a very high one, that of making people
more understanding and sympathetic towards those with
whom in most cases they could not gain any degree of touch,
trying to bridge the jagged gaps that exist between human
beings.' This says more for the novels than they deserve. In
their way they exploit the mining communities just as thoroughly as did the mineowners; they do for class what Hans
Grimm was doing for race in Germany. Lewis Jones, admirable though his organizing and agitatory powers may have
been in life, idealizes the solidarity, courage, doggedness of
the miners for propagandist aims. His reward is the reader's
incredulity. Less overtly political, and far more acutely observed and stylishly written is Gwyn Jones's novel *Times
Like These* (1936). Apart from a disastrous attempt at
phonetic reproduction of the dialect, and a slightly too free
tendency to choose a few 'typical' characters — the agitator,
the rugby international, the pampered wife of the manager—
one gets the impression that this indeed is what it was like in
the late twenties. The authenticity in detail is what confirms
the general conclusion. Mary, back from London, 'thought
of Oliver, Luke and Edgar fetching coal from the tip, and
without putting it to herself in so many words, knew she had
suddenly glimpsed the indomitable spirit of man, here in
these valleys'. The low key captures the contemporary
drabness; there are no heroics, but the order in the novel
itself seems to suggest and correspond to an order and structure in the life of the community. Yet even this novel, faced
with overwhelming evils of the economic situation, doubts
the community's future: 'Indeed to God', he said quietly,
and without profanity, 'what are we in the world for? Everything do seem so useless, somehow.'

The other reaction is to search the past for larger-than-life counters to the despairs of the day. The short years of the mining valleys' exuberance are idealized, not for use but for glory. And they are idealized in two ways; by Jack Jones as a popular chronicler, Richard Llewellyn as a myth-maker. Jack Jones is barely removed from history, Richard Llewellyn takes off from reality into fantasy.

The otherwise admirable study by G.F.Adam[9] tends to over-emphasize the documentary nature of Jack Jones's early novels, or at least, to ascribe to them an over-retrictive documentary intention. One must not be confused by the technique of reportage he sometimes employs; the brief situation reports, the flat recitals of meetings, the truncated heads of speeches, the background information about pit-horses, the head-lining telegraphese of some pages of *Rhondda Roundabout*. These are only devices, sometimes miscalculated perhaps, designed to verify a narrative the main purpose of which is to enclose the history of the Rhondda and of Merthyr in a series of genre·pictures, or more accurately, of 'moral subjects'. Jack Jones is the rough Hogarth of the industrial South.

The Depression created Jack Jones as a writer and his first published novel, *Rhondda Roundabout* (1934) is a cautious rebuilding and dignifying of the community devastated by it. The opening sentences are famous: 'Revolutionary and riotous; religious and musical; sporting and artistic, coal-bearing Rhondda. The starting-point of hunger marches, religious revivals, and Communist miners' delegations to Russia. Place of origin of champion boxers, noted preachers, talented musicians and composers, famous choir conductors, operatic stars and novelists.' The components are the expected ones, but they find their expression more in character than in event. The author himself testifies [10] that he began the book by picking up a piece of paper, making a round ring with a pencil and writing inside it 'Rev. Dan

Price, B.A.' He then went on to make a second ring outside the first, dividing it into six divisions for the six chief supporting characters, and outside that a third ring for another dozen characters. Shoni and Emily, Big Mog and Llew Rhondda do, it is true, illustrate the clichés; but they are the justification of the Rhondda. Jack Jones has comparatively little how-green-was-my-valleying; the flowering is in the people.

Black Parade (1935) and *Bidden to the Feast* (1938) are more specifically historical evocations of Merthyr from about 1880 to 1930. In 1930 he began the chronicle that was to be the basis for these two novels; it was to be called 'Saran' and was to have five parts: the Easy Eighties, the Naughty Nineties, The Birth of a Century, Death's Decade and Depression–Dereliction. It was, he told his wife (*Unfinished Journey*, p.248), 'to reveal the rise, decline and fall of what was . . . the wonder industrial town of the world . . . Today . . . everything's derelict, and Merthyr's a dead town, left high and dry there on the uplands, with about fifteen thousand on the dole.' All was to be shown through his mother, Saran (Sarah Ann), and his family. Against an almost unrelieved background of drunkenness, fighting and squalor we find joy (in Steppwr), self-conquest (in Harry) and fortitude, generosity and natural grace (in Saran, and later in Megan.)

The vitality of the characters, rather than any complexity or subtlety in their presentation, is what carries the novels. They are viewed from the strictest third-person narrator's standpoint; but no-one is in any doubt that narrator and Jack Jones are identified and that they live when he breathes love into them. Sometimes perhaps, and too often in the later works, they become objects of that antiquarian interest that can drown his narrative. Reporter, or local historian? Above all, perhaps, his own biographer. Two long instalments of overt autobiography confirm the fictional use he has already made of his own life in the earlier novels. The characters and incidents in *Unfinished Journey* are scarcely distinguishable from those in *Black Parade* and *Bidden to the Feast;* the family history has been stretched in time in the novels, and filled in by his reading, but it circles around his experience in almost all particulars.

Total recall and boundless enthusiasm for local colour are the elements in Jack Jones's creation of fictional material; sifting has relatively little place. The novels are indifferent imaginative creations, but they are powerful evocations of actual people and places. These are so vividly recalled and so remarkable in themselves that they sometimes acquire an extra dimension: Saran as a Modron figure, Big Mog as Falstaff, Steppwr as Harlequin, Llew Rhondda as, indeed, a leonine figure, Tai-Harry-Blawd as Tom-all-Alone's. Jack Jones falls short of creating a mythology of working-class South Wales, because his vision is too direct, too unselective, too uncompromising. But he peoples the Rhondda and Merthyr with larger than life characters, and gives a sense of those qualities of excess in the society that captured the imagination when exploited by Richard Llewellyn.

Whether we like it or not, the most widely-known representation of Welsh life before *Under Milk Wood* was *How Green was My Valley*. It is, for instance, almost the only twentieth century Anglo-Welsh work not by Dylan Thomas or David Jones to be treated in *Kindlers Literatur Lexikon*[11] as it had been in the Mondadori *Dizionario Universale della letterature contemporanea*[12]. A few sentences from the Kindler article may be translated to convey the sense of the whole: 'Huw thinks of the ordered happy world of his childhood, when the miners and their families lived contently in modest prosperity. He remembers his father, straightforward and full of vitality, accustomed to settling his own affairs and, like a true Welshman, ready to use his fists if this seemed necessary . . . The author is not always able to achieve his intention of having the first-person narrator, whose strong commitment is evident from the beginning, relate the story from the point of view of the various stages of his life. Sometimes the novel is dominated by the nostalgia of a person looking back from an unhappy present to a past seen as idyllic. Nevertheless Llewellyn succeeds in giving a robust and often humorous portrayal of the mining back-ground and the people of Wales . . . The atmospheric effect of the book is strengthened too by the inclusion of the Welsh dialect, without damaging its comprehensibility.'

Two points emerge from the quotation: that the work is taken seriously as literature, and that it has succeeded in imposing its own stereotypes of Welshness (there are other examples of this in the article). This, for many people, is the only Welsh novel.

Richard Llewellyn, to keep to his pen name, came to this novel from an unsettled youth, partly spent in Italy in hotel-kitchens and with a film-unit, and partly in the Army. Out of work in 1931 he cobbled together a living as a bit-player in films, a reporter on a film paper, an assistant director, production manager and eventually playwright. *How Green was My Valley* was based on a draft written while he was with the Army in India (and thus before 1931) and was itself composed in St. David's, Cardiff, London and Llangollen. Published in October 1939 it sold 50,000 copies in four months and over 100,000 when published in America early in 1940,[2] and, no doubt, many hundreds of thousands since then.

It would perhaps be a mistake to base too much speculation on these bald and precarious facts; but it does seem that the genesis of the novel lies farther back than one might have expected. It also appears to have little personal experience behind it. Richard Llewellyn has claimed, in the handbook entry quoted above, that all the characters and incidents have some basis in fact, but are all composite readings. There is certainly not the same personal commitment and reportorial devotion as in Jack Jones. Characters and incidents are chosen for their fictional effect and not because they existed in the living experience of the author.

The mining background is fairly sketchy, though the minimum wage, the sliding scale and the growth of the Union play a part. The physical environment is, of course, prefigured in the title and the paradisal quality of the scenery before the mines came is made a backcloth for semi-rural idyll. One of the most characteristic passages begins 'Our village then, was one of the loveliest you could see. I will say it was lovely, because it was so green and fresh and clean, with wind from off the fields and dews from the mountain.' There follows an account of the narrator tickling trout and then having them for supper: 'My mother used to put them on a hot stone over the fire, wrapped in breadcrumbs, butter, parsley and lemon rind, all bound about with the fresh green leaves of leeks. If there is better food in heaven, I am in a hurry to be there . . . ' And the fundamentally stable nature of the community and the family in the early days is frequently expressed in food and meals. This is the direct expression of nature's sensuous good and the social codifier of a society still fundamentally peasant.

'Shame on you,' Elias shouted . . . 'Profaners of holy days, · what next will you do in your iniquity?'
'Well,' said my father, 'if it is all the same to you, I will have the leg of that goose if Beth will pass the plate.'
But Elias later contributes to the break-up of the family and the community.

The social cohesion of the early days is emphasized in a good number of other ways. One is the community's generosity: the collection for Mrs. Beynon, the sharing of food during the strike. Another is, of course, the singing, of which one example may suffice:

'I looked at the smooth blue sky and the glowing white roofs, the black road, choked with blacker figures of waving men passing down the Hill between groups of women with children clustered about their skirts, all of them flushed by flickering orange lamplight rising in many harmonies, borne upward upon the mists which flew from singing mouths, veiling cold-pinched faces, magnifying the brilliance of hoping eyes, and my heart went tight inside me.

And round about us the Valley echoed with the hymn and lights came out in the farms up on the dark mountain, and down at the pit, and men were waving their lamps, hundreds of tiny sparks keeping time to the beat of the music.
Everybody was singing.
Peace there was again, see.'

(The cinematic organisation of the passage is also something we might note.)
And then the chapels. 'There is good it was to walk to Chapel on a Sunday morning when the sun was shining . . . All the people on the Hill started about the same time.' They all greet one another, the families walk together, and they start singing, and picking up the same hymn until you might think the mountain himself was in song. Then into the Chapel, which 'always smelt the same, of wax, for the woodwork in the gallery and the big seat and pews and pulpit, of soap and water for the stones, of paint a bit, and of hymn books, and camphor from best suits and dresses, and of people, and of smoke from the wood in the stove.'
Embedded in this account is the refrain: 'Beautiful were

the days that are gone, and O, for them to be back.' Even the 'rows of houses where the dross of the collieries lived' merely stress the integration of the true community Huw remembers. The hypocrisy and English-aping of Mr Jonas-Sessions are a betrayal of community demanding retribution; and receiving it at the fists of Dai Bando and Cyfartha Lewis. Justice is simple, and not administered by police or court, but by more direct, not to say primitive means. Even when the old moral certainties have receded primitive justice attempts, appealingly if unavailingly, to reassert itself. Mr Gruffydd has been voted from the chapel by the deacons, seven to three.

'He is going in a sailing ship to Patagonia at the end of the month,' she said. 'He asked them to let him stay till then. But they said he was unclean. Mr. Isaac Wynn.' 'What did Dada say?' I asked her, but not looking. 'Mr. Isaac Wynn is with vinegar plasters,' she said, and trimming her words as with shears, 'and your good father had a bit of an eye from somewhere.'

The simple virtues may be thrown into relief by a running accompaniment of poverty, sickness, and violence, culminating in the ultimate disaster of Huw's father's death, crushed under rock in the mine. But they acquire their aura by being past, and the narrative method employed ensures that the reader knows from the first that they are past, even if the narrator at the end insists that it is 'Thirty years ago, but as fresh, and as near as Now.'

The reader, even within the terms of the narrative, may suspect that memory has heightened golden views: 'It (work in the mines) was different in our time. There was good money and fairness and fair play for all. Not like now.' Social history and social criticism have very minor roles to play here. The more critical reader may go on to feel that the heightening of remembered glories is achieved by a deliberate broadening of the brush-strokes and a coarsening of the emotional quality. These conscious effects are to be seen at their worst in the way the purple passages try to whip up suitable reaction:'My Valley, O my Valley, within me, I will live in you, eternally. Let Death or worse strike this mind and blindness eat these eyes if thought or sight forget you. Valley of the Shadow of Death, now, for some, but not for me, for part of me is the memory of you in your greens and browns, with everything of life happy in your deeps and shades, when you gave sweet scents to us and sent forth spices for the pot, and flowers, and birds sang out for pleasure to be with you.'

The speech rhythms, the inversions, the grammatical idio-syncracies are also exaggerated, though not immoderately. The tacit justification is the apparent (though often not actual) translation of Welsh idiom. 'Go you now'; 'before I will throw you out of the house'; 'there is pleased was my father'; 'I can smell your mother's good bacon from by here, indeed.'; ' "Only talking they are," I said'; ' "Ruth who, were you, before to marry?" I asked her.'

We have all been in all these territories before; in Jack Jones, in Rhys Davies, in Gwyn Jones. Singing, violence, generosity, the emotions and suppressions of Non-conformity, the terrors and the comradeship of the pit, the physical scars of the valleys and the later scars on the lives of the idle thousands. 'Our Davy' has played before in inter-nationals and there have been other fights and fondlings on the mountain. But these were observed more analytically, in more detail, with more qualifications and, no doubt, with more truth.

Richard Llewellyn is not concerned with the truth of the past, but with its fictions, with what we have learned to call 'The poetry of praise'. Coming at the end of the melancholy thirties, with nothing promised except perhaps another Somme, where was there to turn but back? Back to the imagined sources of qualities still partially nourished by the community; to the expanded images and figures whose splendours still implied significance in the wilting contemporary inhabitants of the Valleys.

In many ways we can see through the novel and its conscious artifices, its sentimentalizing, its emotional crudities, its exploitation of what the stranger finds odd about the Welsh. Yet, on our behalf, it has succeeded in superimposing a dream on the South Wales valleys. We cannot see them wholly divorced from its clichés, as we cannot see the Deep South, even in these days, without some echoes of *Uncle Tom's Cabin*. *How Green was My Valley* incorporates the mythology of the Welsh mining community.

NOTES.
1. Beach, J.W., *The Twentieth Century Novel*, New York, 1932, p.421.
2. Vol. III, pp. 236-250.
3.. Evans, E.W., *The Miners of South Wales*, Cardiff, 1961, pp.4-5 and 241; and Morris, J.H. and Williams, L.J., *The South Wales Coal Industry 1841-1875*, Cardiff, 1958, p.73.
4. See Ben Bowen Thomas, *Drych Y Baledwr*, Aberystwyth, 1958, and his *Baledi Morgannwg*, Caerdydd, 1951.
5. Rees, T.Mardy, *Ystoriau Difyr*, Gwrecsam, 1909, and *Difyrwch Gwyr Morgannwg*, Caernarfon, 1916.
6. Davies, D.T.,*Ble Mà Fa?*, Aberystwyth, 1914; translated as *Where is he?*, Stratford, 1917.
7. From his autobiographical *My Struggle for Life*, 1916, p.227, cited on p.127 of Edwards, J.H.K., *The Life and Works of Three Anglo-Welsh writers of East Glamorgan*, Aberystwyth M.A.thesis, 1962, a full and most useful account of Keating, Lewis Jones and Jack Jones.
8. One might add two quotations from Rhys Davies's own evidence in *Twentieth Century Authors, First Supplement*,

ed. Stanley J. Kunitz, New York, 1955, p.26: 'It (the Rhondda Valley) was a turbulent place of high-minded religious disputes, industrial warfare—its riotous strikers were famous —and singing festivals known as Eisteddfods.'
'I try to create my characters first as human beings' i.e. he has not consciously sought to be a regional novelist, though there must remain a Welsh atmosphere to his work.
9. Adam, G.F., *Three Contemporary Anglo-Welsh Regional Novelists: Jack Jones, Rhys Davies and Hilda Vaughan,* Bern, 1949.
10. In *Unfinished Journey,* London, 1937, p.280.
11. In vol.III, Zurich, 1967.
12. In vol.III, Milan, 1961.
13. For the fullest account, see *Twentieth Century Authors,* ed. Stanley J. Kunitz, New York, 1950, p.836.

THE POETRY OF THOMAS PARRY-WILLIAMS

R.Gerallt Jones

There is no doubt that Thomas Parry-Williams is a major figure in twentieth century Welsh literature; neither is there any doubt about the extent of his influence on other writers. Nevertheless, when considering his poetry, one is forced to reassess one's basic concepts about the nature of art and the functions it is best suited to perform. Although often moved to admiration and even a sense of awe by the skill of many individual poems, one is at first left with a feeling of uncertainty and sometimes of bafflement when looking at his work in its totality. I hope to show that this bafflement gives way, the more one reads him, to a realisation that we are in the presence of a great tragic poet.

In direct contrast to his cousin, Robert Williams Parry, one does not feel immediately that here is an undiluted revelation of a poet's personality; there is a caution, a sense of the deliberate balancing of contrary forces, possibly even an unwillingness to accept the real implications of the poet's own most penetrating vision, that, in the final analysis, clouds the issue.

In some ways, he has a good deal in common with his cousin, and with the remainder of that agnostic generation of which he was, after all, a part, a deep and delicate sensitivity, a reserved and modest, even shy personality, and the same feeling of overwhelming uncertainty regarding the

THOMAS PARRY-WILLIAMS

mysteries of creation. But in him there is also an analytic coolness interacting with his poetic sensibility, and a conscious linguistic virtuosity that sometimes threatens to take over altogether. If the function of poetry is to treat of varied subjects with intellectual balance and a high degree of technical skill, then there is no question as to his greatness; if it is to reflect with total commitment the deepest implications of one man's experience and one man's vision, then in spite of one's initial doubts, the greatness remains.

Briefly, he was born in Rhyd-ddu at the foot of Snowdon in 1887, and has limited his literary expression to three kinds of clearly defined literary forms: in poetry, the sonnet and the rhyming couplet, and in prose, a kind of reflective, poetic, self-analytical musing about life under the general heading of 'ysgrif'. (Although his 'ysgrifau' could well be described in some ways as poetry, I will not consider them to be within the scope of this article). He achieved early eminence as a poet by winning both the chair and the crown in National Eisteddfodau in 1912 and 1915, and, in spite of his essentially reserved personality, he has subsequently continued this connection with the National Eisteddfod as an articulate, even sometimes an oratorical, platform adjudicator, and of late years as President of the Eisteddfod Council. After his early eisteddfod successes, during a long tenure of the chair of Welsh at the University College of Wales in Aberystwyth between 1920 and 1952, he published poetry, sometimes in conjunction with 'ysgrifau', in a number of volumes, ranging from *Cerddi* in 1931 to *Myfyrdodau* in 1957, although easily the most significant and substantial of these volumes was the first, and this will repay examination in detail.

It is perhaps significant, however, that he chose to preface a recent record of his poems with a seemingly insignificant little piece called 'Geiriau';

Ni wn ynwir pa hawl a roed i mi
I chwarae campau â'ch hanfodau chwi

A'ch trin a'ch trafod fel y deuai'r chwiw
A throi a throsi'ch gogoniannau gwiw,

Ond wrth ymyrraeth â chwi oll ac un
Mi gefais gip ar f'anian i fy hun.

(I do not know at all what right was given me to play tricks with your natures, to mould and handle you as the urge came, to turn and twist about your marvellous qualities, but as I played around with you one and all I caught a glimpse of my own personality.)

It is not unusual, of course, for a poet to confess a consuming interest in language; but few poets have referred more specifically and more frequently to the process of creation and the nature of words than Parry-Williams, until one gets the feeling that a major part of his motivation in writing is a powerful urge simply to get something down on paper, an overpowering necessity to handle, shape and fashion words for their own sake. It may be a peculiar thing to say about a poet noted in some quarters for his analytic observation of life, but a good deal of the time much of Parry-Williams' poetry gives the impression almost of being 'art for art's sake', a carefully constructed, beautifully fashioned artefact rather than a *cri de coeur*, but also an artefact constructed as the result of a real need to express something; it is not always clear exactly what.

In his sonnet 'Atgno', written in 1931, he regrets the poems that he failed to write, for the impulse only comes in its pristine power once; if it returns to the consciousness it returns only as a pale shadow that can no longer be transformed into poetry. In a poem, 'Ymddiheuriad', which prefaces *Cerddi*, and which is addressed to 'the poems that are not to be found here', he apologises to the rejected poems, which, he says, burnt themselves out before they could properly be caught in words. He says that they came out of somewhere, somehow into his consciousness, 'naked, dis-inherited sparks', that grew into a brief, white-hot fire, only to die away into lifeless dust:

> *Am i chwi losgi'n lludw gan eich nwyd,*
> *Nid dyma'ch lle, wrthodedigion llwyd.*

(Because you burnt yourselves into ashes with your passion, this is not the place for you, grey, rejected ones.)

Is he in fact saying that these embryo poems never actually materialised *because* the initial impetus was so powerful, and so the intellect was never able to grasp and discipline it? Be that as it may, he cannot leave the topic alone, and in 'Ofni', published in *Lloffion* (1942), he expresses the fear that these urges to write that have so far driven him on are growing less powerful and more infrequent:

> *Y mae arnaf ofn, nid oes dim dau,*
> *Fod yr hen gyffroadau'n dechrau prinhau*

(I'm afraid, there's no two ways about it, that the old excite-ments are growing fewer.)

He recites the way in which his sensibilities are less sharp than they were, and the feeling he has that he has exper-ienced all that he is destined to experience, and yet, he says at the end, there was clearly some creative impulse behind his desire to write of the fears themselves. In the same volume, two other poems, 'Temtasiwn' and 'Awen', treat of the same topic in different ways, 'Temtasiwn' seemingly concerned with a passing desire to write free-and-easy verse and 'Awen' with the basic impulses of creative activity. Once again, in another poem entitled 'Awen' in his 1949 volume, *Ugain o Gerddi*, he writes of the need to write, and the fact that some innate inhibition time and again prevents embryo poems from coming to fruition. In this poem too he expresses his continuing fear that the urge to write will die away, and that the creative process will cease:

> *Cyn i'r hwrdd fynd heibio, mi fentraf ar gân neu ddwy*
> *Eto, rhag ofn na ddaw blas ar ganu mwy.*
>
> *Mae rhyw aflwydd byth a hefyd yn tarfu dyn,*
> *A chyn eu geni'n tagu'r caneuon bob un,*
>
> *A'r hyn a elwir yn Awen yn colli nodd,*
> *Ac yn amlach na pheidio'n erthylu, gwaetha'r modd.*

(Before the mood pass, I'll chance a poem or two once again, in case the feeling for writing doesn't come any more. Some failing all the time frustrates a man and chokes all the poems before they are born, and that which we call inspiration loses its sap, and more often than not aborts, worst luck.)
So, he says, he will clutch at a favourable moment and write 'to loosen the tension of the tightness in my breast'. He then lists a number of possible topics - titles which are in fact represented by poems in *Ugain o Gerddi* - but he ends, as in so many poems, on a falling cadence, by saying that once again some interruption has cut across his mood and the inspiration has disappeared.

Taken all in all, although some of these poems need not be considered all that seriously, we do find here a creative artist wrestling with the frustrations of his calling. His need to write is obvious; his motivation comes, as with all poets surely, in fits and starts; his interest in words as instruments and as malleable entities is intense, but he harps on the difficulties of creation and the difficulties of actually finding words for the vague and insubstantial forms that hover in his mind. His rather petulant complaint in 'Temtasiwn' betrays the fact that he is not one who finds writing easy. The truth seems to be that his complex and ambivalent reactions to human experience, not informed by any one consuming message like, for example, that which informed the poetry of his colleague in the Welsh department at Aberystwyth, Gwenallt, but rather by the tentative uncertainties of an intelligent and sensitive human being faced by the cruelties and ironies of life, simply made it difficult for him to know what to make of it, and therefore, ultimately, what to say in his poems.

Often, therefore, and not surprisingly, he takes refuge in constructing finely-turned verse, and there is no doubt that he has an unrivalled mastery of his medium, on topics that allow him to make civilised comments at one remove from his subject, without being totally involved himself. Poems like 'Dic Aberdaron' and 'Y Bilidowcars' from *Ugain o Gerddi* fall into this category, fanciful, humorous and full of acute observation of the surface of life, but not, to use Coleridge's distinction between 'imagination' and 'fancy', plumbing the depths of his imaginative capabilities. My own feeling is that a number of his best-known sonnets, justly prized for their balance and verbal beauty, 'Dychwelyd', for example, come into this category, taking, as they do, one basic idea, which in 'Dychwelyd' is the insignificance of human life compared with the vast interstellar spaces, and developing it verbally rather than intellectually.

But fundamentally, of course, he is no decorative versifier. He is a poet of great gifts wrestling with an uncertain, clouded vision. If we are to get a clearer idea of the true nature of this vision, we must look at the background from which he came, a background that has played a massive part in modern Welsh literature.

It is clearly something more than coincidence that such a large proportion of the Welsh literature written during this century has sprung from a few square miles of territory, having as their centre the dominating precipices of Snowdon. That part of Gwynedd which has always been inhospitable to inquisitive strangers, from Archbishop Baldwin to George Borrow, and never remotely accessible to conquerors, is a grim and unrelenting landscape, suggestive of a mountainous country far bigger in scope and far higher in altitude than in fact Snowdonia is. The whole area, of course, has been associated with legend and folk history from earliest times, but it seems that during the last forty years a disproportionate concentration of Welsh literary output has emanated from here. Perhaps it is not over-fanciful to suggest that this is some kind of cultural parallel to the periodic retreats into Snowdonia that took place during Norman times, when the great princes of Gwynedd expanded their territories far and wide into Powys Ceredigion, and even Dyfed and Deheubarth, only to be pushed back time and again to their starting-point of West Gwynedd which, by and large, they never lost. At a time of intense cultural pressures on the Welsh language, it may be natural that it should turn for refreshment to its ancient source of strength.

On Snowdon's periphery to the north-west is Rhosgadfan. Kate Roberts has written in story after story of the grim struggle for survival that took place there in a country where the rock barely gives way to a thin crust of poor soil. A little lower down the same slopes, John Gwilym Jones examines in his plays the psychological complexities of a village community which attempts to relate ancient habits of mountain living to the middle-class bourgeois values of the small town and the coast. Further north, as we have already seen, Robert Williams Parry feared from a distance the remote power of the mountains, preferring the precarious safety of woodland and pasture in the no-man's-land between the Carneddi and the sea. At the foot of

Snowdon itself, T.Rowland Hughes looked upwards from the village of Llanberis, surrounded by the huge scars of open-cast slate quarries, and attempted in his novels to re-create a society that was forced to survive in the dangerous shadow of the only incursion that the Industrial Revolution ever made into these mountains.

But it was Thomas Parry-Williams, born at Rhyd-ddu on the south-western slopes, who faced the implications of this strange land head-on and, obsessed by the relationship between man and his natural environment, spent his whole life as a writer trying to analyse and dismember his obsession. A good deal has been written about his poetry of late and much has been made both of his intellectual eminence and many academic distinctions, and also of his paganistic/nihilistic/pessimistic philosophy. There can, of course, be no doubt about the striking brilliance of his early academic career, spanning universities as far apart as Wales and Germany, and subjects as unrelated as Linguistics and Medicine. Neither can there be any argument about the spectacular competitive successes which have by now become a part of Eisteddfodic legend. But there can equally be no doubt that he basically rejected the pursuit of superficial versatility, and saw his early successes clearly enough for what they were, the restless searchings of a highly talented but immature mind.

I well remember his reply to an interviewer's interview-question regarding his pessimism/paganism. He said in effect that anyone who expected a consistent philosophy in the body of a poet's work had the wrong idea both about poetry and about human beings. He went on to say that what one was most likely to gather from the totality of a man's poetry was the inconsistency of human beings and the way in which the nature of experience was swayed and generated by moods and feelings of the moment and that he himself was quite capable of expressing dark despair one moment and a positive assertion of life the next. In this, he seems to express the essence of his art, for like his cousin, Robert Williams Parry, what pervades his best work is the total and often agonising honesty of his reaction to a particular experience, without any real attempt to slot it into a consistent philosophical or intellectual framework.

And so, naturally enough, we have poems like 'Dychwelyd', when he simply expresses his feeling that man's life is but a 'ripple in time, or shadow of a scar' on the vast stillness and imperturbability of the earth itself. Man's existence is to him, on these occasions, an insignificant and meaningless interruption of the regular cycle of natural events. At other times, he can see great significance in a tiny symbolic experience, such as the glimpse of an owl sitting on a telegraph pole which suddenly and inexplicably brings home to him aspects of terror and mystery in the universe at a time when he had felt most at home in familiar surroundings. I cannot think that this kind of ambivalence in any way reflects either on his intelligence or on his perception, but represents, more truly than any attempt at a consistent philosophy, his concept of the poet's function. At the root of existence, as another mystic poet, Waldo Williams, said, is a paradox and it is this basic fact, and the recognition of it, which distinguishes the agonising search for truth of the genuine artist from the manufactured fabric of the second rate. The true distinction of Thomas Parry-Williams at his best lies in the clarity with which he tries to examine and live with this paradox. Life is insignificant, but it is also full of significant moments; man is rational, but his greatest experiences are born, not of logical discoveries, but of brief flashes of irrational inspiration whose roots lie deep in mystery. Even in moments of deepest despair, man fights for the enduring vision which makes life not only worthwhile but intensely inspiring. For a broader insight into the nature of the paradox as Parry-Williams sees it, I believe we must examine again more carefully the nature of the square mile which has so often been the subject of his contemplation.

Paradoxes abound in this locality. For Parry-Williams, his childhood was dominated by the contrast between the cold vastness of the mountain and the warm confines of family life in the schoolhouse at Rhyd-ddu. Above was the huge, incomprehensible mass of ancient rock which some-how or other had woven itself into the fabric of his being. Below was the small, straggling, almost irrelevant village, isolated and with no obvious reason for its existence. At the centre of this village, for him, was the only place where warmth and security were to be found, his home. The contrast is obvious between the vast inaccessibility of the one and the easily understood closeness of the other; the paradox lies in his equally magnetic attachment to both. To over-simplify, it might be said that his attachment to what was clearly a sheltered home background was an escape from the terror generated by his realisation that unanswerable questions were posed by his relationship with the mountain.

In a famous sonnet, 'Moelni', he expresses his feeling of affinity with the smooth contours of the mountain in its purest and simplest form. He tells us how there was nothing but a barren, treeless world around his birthplace, 'as though giants had long been polishing the slopes', and he describes how he felt the shapes of those slopes pressing in upon him during his childhood until they became a part of his being:

Ymwasgai hen ffurf y mynyddoedd hyn,
Nes mynd o'u moelni i mewn i'm hanfod i.

Having built up the octet of the sonnet (and he certainly thinks of his poems in this careful, constructionist way) with a sentiment deeply reminiscent of Wordsworth's 'Prelude', then he imagines, in the sestet, not for the last time

71

in his poems, some part of him remaining in the world after his departure, being discovered by a friend whose affinity with the mountain is similar to his own, and being found to have no shape or form but the barren smoothness of the rock itself.

In another sonnet, 'Tynfa', he expresses exactly the same feeling in connection with the River Gwyrfai;

> *Os ydyw Afon Gwyrfai wedi troi*
> *Duwch ei dyfroedd trwy fy ngwaedlif i*

(If the River Gwyrfai has diverted the course of its dark waters into my bloodstream) and compares the way in which the river starts, moves through and leaves the mountain country without ever in fact leaving it, with his own parallel experience:

> *mae'r fan a roes*
> *Ein cychwyn gyda'n gilydd, yn parhau*
> *Ynglŷn wrth ein crwydriadau . . .*

(The place that gave us both our starting-point, continues bound to our wanderings,) and he touches here on a common theme, that he carries his locality and its nature bound up with him wherever he goes.

Very often, his consideration of the locality with which his experiences are bound up is linked with considerations of the duality within his own personality, and it is here that he brings in his emotional ties with his home and family. In the sonnet, 'Gweddill', he traces the traits he has inherited from his parents, and speaks of his father's gifts of self-expression and his mother's impassioned nature, and of how he has treasured this personal heritage. Then he describes their departure in one of those superbly comprehensive lines that shine out like stars in all his poems,

> *Gan newid hen gynefin am y gro*

(Exchanging an old familiar environment for the hard soil) and reminds himself that while verse and passion remain in him he thereby keeps alive some part of them.

And then, in sonnet after sonnet, he stresses the duality and ambiguity of man's reactions to life, an ambiguity made up, in 'Argyhoeddiad', of the contrast between man's occasional feeling, as he stands on the mountainside, that he is in truth lord of creation, and the real truth is that he is in fact as much in the grip of huge, irrational forces as the pebble that he himself throws down the slope and watches bouncing and careering its way to the bottom. In 'Dylluan', he contrasts the homely familiarity of his immediate surroundings with the sudden fear created by the sight of an owl. In 'Gorffwys', he begins by expressing a mood of lassitude and lethargy and then describes the way in which the uneasiness and discontent of his searching mind takes over as the tiredness fades, and the poem ends in an expression of active and compulsive energy.

In a fine sonnet called 'Sialens', he fights against the imminent incursion of 'middle-age' - a bogey that carries with it thoughts of diminished sensitivity and passion:

> *Gwae fi o'm tynged, oni ddringaf i*
> *I ben y clogwyn draw a dodi llef*
> *Yn erbyn yr ysbeilwyr.*

(Let my fate be cursed, unless I climb to the head of that crag there and cry out against these vandals.) He proclaims his belief that by resisting he can keep his sensibilities alive:

> *dof yn ieuanc rydd,*
> *Mi wn, o'r sgarmes fawr, pan ddêl ei dydd.*

(I shall emerge young and free, I know, from that great battle, when the day comes.) This is a rare piece of stark,

73

optimistic realism in some ways paralleled by Dylan Thomas's 'rage, rage, against the dying of the light.'

More and more, however, as we read these sonnets, loving in their attitude to his parents in 'Tŷ'r Ysgol', 'Ofn' and in other poems in other volumes, awe-struck in their view of Eryri in 'Moelni', 'Dychwelyd', 'Tynfa', affectionate in their view of Rhyd-ddu in 'Llyn y Gadair' and 'Dylluan', we see that the prevailing mood is sombre and the prevailing themes are the inevitability of old age, and death, and an all-pervading sense of human insufficiency, deepening as the poet grows older. In the sonnet, 'Y Rheswm', written in 1930, there is a calm but clear manifestation of this.

The sonnet begins with a cinematic picture of a dead branch drooping from a living summer tree, shedding its leaves ahead of time:

Yn efelychu'r hydref yn yr haf

(Imitating autumn in summer). Then he continues the picture by comparing the summer mist on the slopes of Pen-y-Cefn with winter snow. But it is not because of these things, in the 'dog days', that a cold, strange sense of loss can be heard in his voice, it is because this peculiar inseason, out-of-season feeling in the world of nature is reflected in his own aging personality:

Ond am fod ynof fis Gorffennaf ffôl
Yn ciprys gydag Ebrill na ddaw'n ôl.

(But because there is in me a stupid July fighting with an April that will never come back.)

If we get this sense of ultimate tragedy peeping through sonnets which are by and large written in a mood of contemplative quietness, we get it even more clearly in some of the short series of poems, 'O Ddyddlyfr Taith', which were the result of a long sea voyage to South America. Some of these are merely occasional poems, but a genuine sense of strangeness and mystery underlies most of them, particularly so the ballad-type 'Y Ferch ar y Cei yn Rio', and this prepares us for two poems of greater significance in this group, one a perfectly formulated lyric, describing the funeral at sea of an old man. It is a classical expression of stoic observation, and worth quoting in full:

> *Aeth henwr heno ryw bryd tua saith*
> *I ddiwedd ei siwrnai cyn pen y daith*
>
> *Gwasanaeth, gweddi, sblais ar y dŵr,*
> *A phlanciau gweigion lle'r oedd yr hen ŵr.*
>
> *Daeth fflach o oleudy Ushant ar y dde,*
> *A Seren yr Hwyr i orllewin y ne',*
>
> *A rhyngddynt fe aeth hen ŵr at ei Iôr*
> *Mewn sachlen wrth haearn trwy waelod y môr.*

(Tonight about seven an old man came to his journey's end before the voyage was complete/a service, a prayer, a splash on the water, and empty planks where the old man had been./ A flash came from Ushant lighthouse on the right, and the Evening Star to the western sky,/ And between them an old man went to his maker in ironbound sackcloth through the bottom of the sea.) The laconic simplicity of this description is Parry-Williams at his most telling, but there is another poem in this group that is grimmer and harsher still. It is entitled 'Carchar' and expresses a momentary revulsion against the whole strange environment he finds himself in and in particular the strangeness of different races and unfamiliar people, and he ends this poem by asking for licence not to have to attempt a Christian tolerance towards the people he sees around him:

> *Gad imi ennyd, O Arglwydd Dduw,*
> *Gasáu dy greadigaethau Di.*

(Let me for a moment, O Lord God, hate your creations.)

At other times, coming back home, he mixes this kind of hardness with a more intimate personal involvement, often, however, affecting the same kind of balance of attitudes, or ambiguity of reactions, that we have found in many of the sonnets. He seems to be attempting to reflect within the same poem both the emotional content of an experience and a rational comment upon it.

In the poem, 'Hon', he proceeds to attack the usual manifestations of patriotism:

> *Peidiwch, da chwi,*
> *A chlegar am uned a chenedl a gwlad o hyd:*
> *Mae digon o'r rhain, heb Gymru, i'w cael yn y byd.*

(For God's sake stop prattling of unit and nation and land all the time. There's plenty of these, without Wales, to be found in the world).
He then goes on to say, however, that his place of escape is not somewhere outside Wales but Snowdonia itself:

> *'Here's Snowdon and its crew; here's the land, bleak and bare;*
> *Here's the lake and river and crag, and look, over there,*
> *The house where I was born.'*

The sudden experience of being transported in imagination into his native environment undermines the certainty of his earlier criticisms:

> *'But see, between the earth and the heavens,*
> *All through the place there are voices and apparitions.'*

The only thing that gives meaning to patriotism, as far as he is concerned, is his relationship with Eryri, his home. In spite of the statement with which he ends the poem,

> *'And I feel the claws of Wales tearing at my heart.*
> *God help me, I cannot get away from this spot,'*

his earlier attack on the noises of patriotism remains valid and remains a genuine expression of an attitude he expresses more than once.

The kind of ambivalence shown in this poem is seen again in another, 'Carol Nadolig', where he begins by berating Death for coming at an inapposite time to take away his father's life.

> *A hell of a thing for Death on that holiday*
> *To come like Father Christmas on his way,*
>
> *And take him from us, and with a single stroke*
> *Turn the Feast of Birth to a Feast of Death, as a joke.'*

This is the authentic voice of the stoic who is in fact taking the Shakespearean view that men are as 'flies to wanton boys' and most of the poem is a powerful variation on this theme. However, he ends, unexpectedly on the surface, by describing the way in which:

> *'I saw him come from the glen with his summons a later day,*
> *One Sunday morning to gather my mother to his breast.*
> *I lost my head: I take back my words.'*

But, of course, the ambivalance is superficial. The retraction, in this poem as in 'Hon' is ironic. The poet must know full well that the soft words of the final couplet make no difference to the bitter attack contained in the remainder of the poem. As in 'Hon', a cool reconsideration of the facts leads him to regret his original outburst of emotion, and whereas in 'Hon' he admits that there are elements which are valid, underlying the jingoistic claptrap that he detests, so in this poem, having given way to a natural and viciously expressed bitterness at the way in which death became a spectre at the feast he then regains his composure and qualifies his anger both by expressing the view that we have little right to question the way in which Death goes about his business and also by accepting that its effects are the same in any case. For the reader, however, both standpoints are valid and it is the sense of fairness which impels Parry-Williams to include both moods within the compass of the same poem that gives his work genuine quality when he is commenting on life at large.

As Gwyn Thomas noted in a *Poetry Wales* review of the recent collected edition of Parry-Williams's poetry, it is very difficult to make meaningful comments about style when one is referring to work that can only be read in translation. But it must at least be said that the phenomenal and conscious development in Parry-Williams's style between his early work, dated and inflated and cruelly quoted in a recent book by Dyfnallt Morgan, and the kind of language used in the poems we have just been discussing forms an integral part of the impact made by his comments on the cruelties and ironies of life. The whole of 'Carol Nadolig' is couched in colloquial language purified in the Wordsworthian sense, by its being sculpted within a tight rhythmic framework and ruthlessly shorn of any frivolities. There can be no poet in the language who has succeeded so well in giving the impression of using spoken vernacular while at the same time using high technical skill in framing memorable rhyming couplets. The secret is twofold; it lies in his utter familiarity with the very fabric of language itself which enables him both to invent and to use words from far and wide which give an immediate impact both in their sound and sense and in his inimitable feel for poetic rhythms that is well enough known in his celebrated reading of his own poetry. Let us consider two couplets in 'Carol Nadolig':

Dyna gythraul o beth oedd i'r Angau ar fore'r ŵyl
Ddod heibio fel Ffaddar Crismas o ran rhyw hwyl

A mynd ag ef oddi arnom, ac ar un strôc
Droi Gŵyl y geni'n Ddygwyl y Marw, fel jôc.

In these couplets, as in all his other poems in this metre, he has taken what used to be a medium for light-hearted ballad-type versifying, the *rhigwm,* and made it into a medium for hard comment simply by virtue of the tightness of the language. In the first line, 'cythraul o beth' is a totally authentic colloquial version of 'a hell of a thing', whereas 'Angau', especially with a capital letter, and 'gwyl' are formal and dignified terms for death and Christmas. Then in the second line he has taken what has come to be an unfortunate tendency in spoken Welsh, the gallicising of a totally English expression, and transcribed it literally, simply by adapting the spelling, in the term 'Ffaddar Crismas'. The final phrase of this line, 'o ran rhyw hwyl' is an innocent, bald statement meaning simply 'for fun'. Having built up the structure like this, he ends the four lines with a telling antithesis and caps it with the sort of resounding rhyme which he uses sparingly but always with maximum effect. When one bears in mind that practically every line of what appears on the surface to be a smooth jingle is constructed as carefully as this, it may be possible to imagine something of the contribution that conscious stylistic effects have had on his work.

In all these poems we find that the familiar people and the familiar mountains of his home are the enduring realities. It is for them that he reserves his love. All that lies outside this ill-matched marriage between the aloof geological form-ation and the warm recollection of family is open to question. These two remain the permanent touchstones of experience.

For all his attempts to dilute and balance his comments on life, there are occasions when a dark, tragic vision presents itself in an intensely passionate form, nowhere more so than in three poems published consecutively in *Cerddi,* and these three, to my mind, constitute a final proof of his greatness as a tragic poet.

'Yr Esgyrn Hyn' emphasises the corruption all flesh is heir to and deliberately creates a stark contrast between the joyful liveliness and optimism of young love and the physical decay of death. He starts by asking a simple question:

> *Beth fyddi dithau, ferch, a myfi,*
> *Pan gilio'r cnawd o'r hyn ydym ni?*

(And what will you be, girl, and me, when the flesh fades from what we are?) And he answers the question in a series of horrific descriptions of a skeleton:

> *Nid erys dim o'r hyn wyt i mi,—*
> *Dim ond dy ddannedd gwynion di.*
> *Ni bydd ohonom ar ôl yn y byd*
> *Ond asgwrn ac asgwrn ac asgwrn mud;*
>
> *Dau bentwr bach dan chwerthinog ne',*
> *Mewn gorffwys di-gnawd, heb na bw na be.*

(Nothing will remain of what you are to me, nothing but your white teeth./ There will be nothing left of us in the world but bone and bone and silent bone:/ Two little heaps beneath a laughing heaven in fleshless rest with no sound or protest.)

Laugh on, he says, and enjoy your life while you can, because it won't last long, and then he finishes by evoking a further comparison between the freshness of youth and an image familiar enough to him, that of a putrefying carcase, watched by birds of prey, somewhere high up on the windy slopes:

Asgwrn ac asgwrn, forwynig wen,
A chudyll a chigfran uwch dy ben;

Heb neb yn gofyn i'r pedwar gwynt:
'P'le mae'r storm o gwawd a fu iddi gynt?'

('Bone and bone, my beautiful girl, and the hawk and the raven over your head:— With no-one to ask the four winds 'Where is the storm of flesh that was once hers?')

In *Cerddi*, 'Yr Esgyrn Hyn' is sandwiched between two other very similar poems on similar themes, 'Dwy Gerdd', written in 1922, and 'Celwydd', written in 1924. He begins 'Dwy Gerdd' with a bleak statement to the one who is the recipient of the three poems that all is falsehood and deception:

Dy dwyllo'r ydwyf: twyllwyr ydym oll
Heb eithrio'r un.

(I'm deceiving you: we are all deceivers, with no exceptions.) The remainder of the first part of this poem is a series of antitheses, all tending towards the grim view that there is no truth, no validity, no tangible reality. His loved one, he says, sometimes succeeds in creating the impression that she can fill the void:

Dy felltith ydyw'r ddawn a roed i ti
I lenwi'r gwagle â thydi dy hun.

(Your curse is the talent given you to fill the vacuum with your own self.) But this too, he says in the next stanza, is a deception; all appearances are false and all hopes of permanence dissolve like drops of rain.

> *Nid yw'r gwir ond gau,*
> *A bywyd nid yw fyw i minnau mwy.*
> *Gwrando ar anniddigrwydd dafnau'r glaw, —*
> *Ffurfiau dros dro ŷm ninnau, yn disgwyl fel hwynt-hwy.*

(Truth is but falsehood, and life is no longer alive for me. Listen to the raindrop's discontent - we too are forms that pass, waiting just like them.) And then he looks back at their experiences together, and his nihilism in turn is shaken by the clarity of memory and the intensity of existential certainties:

> *Ac eto yr oedd Medi'n Fedi'n wir,*
> *Ac Arfon yn fynyddoedd dan ein traed,*
> *Y niwl yn niwl, ac un ac un yn ddau,*
> *Ac awr ac awr yn oriau, tithau'n gig a gwaed.*

(And yet September was in truth September, and Arfon was mountainous beneath our feet, the mist was mist and one and one made two, hour to hour made hours and you were flesh and blood.)
And yet even this is insubstantial, for experience, once gone, cannot be recaptured, nor can its reality be guaranteed; everything passes, all is uncertain and, once again, there is no tangible reality:

> *Nid yw Medi ond mis,*
> *A hwnnw'n darfod, a heb fod erioed.*
> *Nid oes yn Arfon heddiw i mi, sy'mhell,*
> *Fynydd na niwl na dim ond ffurfiau'n cadw oed.*

(September is only a month, a month that ends, and without ever having been. There isn't in Arfon today for me, who is far away, either mountain or mist or anything but forms that meet.)

Having then gone on to confess that she does not share this sense of emptiness, strikingly expressed in the tenuous balance of opposites from line to line in the poem, he ends the first part with a statement of qualified, but incomprehensible, optimism. This whole section, in its emphasis on the terrible gulf between appearance and reality, and its deep distress at the impossibility of discovering the nature of truth, much as the poet wants to believe in the enduring reality of his loved one, is a powerful statement.

The second part of the poem is a beautifully written, but not altogether satisfactory, synthesis of the insoluble problems posed in the first part. 'I deceived you,' he says, 'when I said I was a deceiver . . . the flesh of your hand was true substance.' And he describes their experiences together as interwoven with that suspended moment in time when the experience took place, and held forever in the memory as part of an enduring landscape:

> *Ac yno mae'r clogwyni, a'r niwl yn niwl,*
> *A Medi'n Fedi o hyd, ac un ac un yn ddau.*

(And there the crags are, and the mist is mist, September still September, and one and one make two.)

In this strange, contorted poem one somehow feels that the agonised searching after reality of the first part, with the repetition that emphasises the poet's lonely sense of having lost his way, rings more truly than the romantic fusion of a second part that seems in the context of the whole to be no more than a desperate clutching after straws. This feeling is intensified when we read the undiluted bitterness of 'Yr Esgyrn Hyn', and then go on to read 'Celwydd', written in 1924 and the final poem of the trilogy.

Again, the theme is the impossibility of discovering truth

either in the static framework of time and created things, or in the moving pattern of human relationships. He begins, as ever, even in his most desperate expressions of doubt, with the utter confidence of the master craftsman handling a medium he understands, with a couplet of classic simplicity:

> *Daeth Haf Bach Mihangel trwy weddill yr ŷd,*
> *Yn llond ei groen ac yn gelwydd i gyd.*

(The Indian summer moved through the stubble of the corn, full of himself and all lies.)
He says he knows him for a liar because he himself practises the same brand of deceit. And then he admits a glimmer of hope:

> *Weithiau — mewn breuddwyd — daw fflach o'r gwir,*
> *Ond wedyn anwiredd a thwyllo hir.*

(Sometimes— in a dream— comes a flash of truth, but then untruth and long deceit.) And this is followed by a terrible statement that carries an air of finality:
> *Trech ydyw'r nos na'r goleuddydd clir.*

(Night conquers the clear light of day.)
The second section of this four-part poem is given over to a straight condemnation of the lying and cheating he feels to be implicit in any loving relationship:

> *Gwae nad oes gwir! Ni bu rhyngom ein dau*
> *Ond cusanau celwyddog a geiriau gau.*

(Alas that there is no truth. There has never been anything between us two but lying kisses and false words.)
In the third section he sees the pride of youthful flesh as laughable, as indeed he also sees it in 'Yr Esgyrn Hyn', and

he once again contemplates the decay of physical excellence in a fine, sad couplet:

> *Ac yntau'n aros ar ddiwedd ei rawd*
> *I edrych yn ôl dros adfeilion cnawd,*

(And he pauses at the end of his journey to look back on the ruins of his flesh,)

Looking back, he sees nothing there, beneath the putre-faction, but 'desire and death and sin and fear', and of the four, death is the mightiest:

> *Ac angau'n traflyncu'r lleill yn syth,*
> *Gan wneuthur y gwegi'n wacath fyth.*

(And death immediately swallows up the others, making the emptiness emptier still.)

In the last section, he stand back from his deep personal involvement, an involvement that has been expressed in reverberating oratory, and coldly reviews the whole chaotic mess that is man's life on earth, in a series of couplets that would compare with any poetic expression in any language as a crystallisation of the sheer unrelieved absurdity of life:

> *Gwae ni ein dodi ar dipyn byd*
> *Ynghrog mewn ehangder sy'n gam i gyd,*
>
> *A'n gosod i gerdded ar lwybrau nad yw*
> *Yn bosib eu cerdded — a cheisio byw;*
>
> *A'n gadael i hercian i gam o gam*
> *Rhwng pechod ac angau heb wybod paham;*

(Woe that we should be put on this bit of a world, hanging in a vacuum that is all crooked,/ set to tread paths that can't be trodden, and told to try and live;/ and left to limp, step by step, from sin to death without knowing why;)

These three poems, taken together form the most powerful expression of Parry-Williams's dark and sombre vision of a crazy, inverted, absurd universe within which man has to attempt some kind of meaningful stab at existence.

In these three poems the vision is largely unrelieved, except in one part of 'Dwy Gerdd', by any attempt to balance it with a cool application either of rationality or of that mystic appeal to the eternal beneficence of his home environ-ment that we find in some of the sonnets. (It is noticeable, however, and in many ways typical of his reluctance to accept the starkness of his vision, that to each of these poems he has attached a sub-heading or alternative title; 'Yr Esgyrn Hyn' he dubs 'a momentary fancy', 'Celwydd' he sub-titles 'a dark hour', and he gives 'Dwy Gerdd' the accolade of an introductory jingle, 'it speaks darkly of something that came into my understanding once and then disappeared. I don't know what it was, and what does it matter?' It is all a vain attempt to pass jewellery off as paste.Nothing can dispel the sense of dark power that pervades these poems, nor can we be convinced that they express anything but Parry-Williams's deepest convictions at the time when they were written.)

I do not see Thomas Parry-Williams as an analytic observer of life, nor as a scholarly intellectual bringing wide areas of knowledge to bear on his verse. I see him, as I see his cousin, a human being looking out onto a dark world with a fearful courage, a man forced to express his bafflement and lack of ultimate hope, but one who, by the force of his craft and the sheer honesty of his approach in his best poems, achieves a tragic intensity in his bitter condemnation of the absurdities of life. The saving grace is the passion, the deep compassion; the poetry, as for Wilfred Owen, is in the pity. He speaks explicitly more than once of the absolute value of compassion, of the need for tears. Tears, to some extent, relieve the anguish; a sympathetic view of the absurd incongruities of the universe is the most that can be ex-pected. And so it may be right to conclude a consideration of his verse, not with 'Celwydd', or with 'Dychwelyd', or with the tempered bitterness of 'Carol Nadolig', but with an early, simple lyric that sings of the inexplicable tears of a sensitive youth face to face with the universe.

Duw a ŵyr beth oedd fy nagrau,
Ef ei Hun oedd biau'r lli;
Wylwn am fod rhaid i'r Duwdod
Wrth fy negrau i.

(God knows what my tears were, He himself owned that flood; I wept because the godhead needed my tears.)
I believe that T.H.Parry-Williams is in the final assessment a great poet because the simple innocence of that response always and inevitably underpins any cerebral attempt to analyse the peculiarities of life; the analysis never penetrates the mystery and the poet's wonder remains.

SEEING ETERNITY: VERNON WATKINS
AND THE POET'S TASK

Leslie Norris

The work of any poet demands, to a greater or lesser degree, a special set of critical tools designed for that work alone; for poets do not roll identically from the conveyor belt equipped with the same starter motors and identical styling. Generally, perhaps, we can assume some basic attitudes, some rules of thumb; but this is least possible for the critic approaching the poetry of Vernon Watkins. He himself, although a notably tolerant and kindly man, had little time for critics. 'For the lyric poet, what better critic than silence?'[1] he asked, and a more scathing comment was 'critics, even unimportant ones, are bound to demonstrate their vitality, like sandhoppers'.[2]

Yet his methods and to some extent his material are so uncommon in our time that his work demands a peculiarly sensitive and sympathetic commentator. Practised as we are in appraising what is fashionable and popular, it may be that we find work as unusual as Watkins's does not respond to our normal methods. This, of course, is not to suggest that Watkins has been uniformly unlucky in his critics. Among others Kathleen Raine has been a splendid advocate on his behalf, and recently Roland Mathias has shown himself one of the most vigorous and constructive of Watkins's supporters.[4]

Nor is this essay an attempt to establish myself as that ideal critic I have posited; far from it. All I can do is to try to establish those areas of Watkins's concern which seem to me to be present in his work from the beginning, and which strengthen and develop as the poet grew in confidence and control.

Watkins was not unhelpful in this direction. Central to his philosophy was the experience he suffered as a young man, an experience which changed the direction of his thought. Both Gwen Watkins and Kathleen Raine compare it to that suffered by St. Paul on the road to Damascus, a period of intense stress followed by enlightenment. Since Watkins was always and unquestioningly a Christian, it was not a specifically religious enlightenment that came to him. Rather was it with exciting certainty the real nature of Time and Eternity. He destroyed all the poems he had written up to this time, since they were, he realised, untruthful. 'It took several years for my style to catch up with this experience, so powerful were the verbal legacies left me by the poets I had admired for so long. I now saw them in a new light, *but I could not translate my transfigured vision of the world into language.*'[5] The italics are mine; I have emphasised the initial nature of Watkins's task.

Diffidently at first, and then with growing assurance and understanding, Watkins began to explore and interpret the eternal world of his vision. There were hints in *Ballad of the Mari Lwyd*, mainly in the use of symbols. The sycamore tree, for example, in the weak little poem 'Autumn Song' or more positively in 'Sycamore', is seen to be a symbol of the defeat of time, an example of something near timelessness. Not only is it a particularly long-lived tree, but it achieves a kind of immortality through the high fertility of its keys, and its wood is used to make musical instruments and carvings, works of art—again a means of immortality, and one which Yeats, Watkins's master, had explored in the

'Byzantium''poems and in 'Lapis Lazuli'. The sycamore also has a further importance since it was into the branches of a sycamore tree that Zachaeus[6] climbed in order to see Christ pass, and there he received his vision of the eternal world which changed his whole life. Zachaeus, 'that short-statured man', is obviously a person with whom Watkins can identify, and the sycamore tree is linked with this identification.

This relationship is more closely examined in 'Zachaeus in the Leaves' (from *The Lady with the Unicorn*), a poem in which Watkins attempts to recreate the experience of the chief of the publicans and to relate the interdependence of Christianity and myth. But it should not be forgotten that there are many other significant symbols, particularly those which employ the Platonic image of water, either as stream or fountain, perpetually flowing and perpetually renewed. These, too, suggest to us an eternal world.

What Watkins came to believe, then, was something like this. Firstly, that time does not exist. This he took as a simple and Christian truth. He did not have to invent the gyres of Yeats or any other complexities; rather it was a simple and unblemished faith like that of Vaughan or Blake. There existed, he felt, a perfect world of which this world was only a flawed copy. This he first suggested in 'Prime Colours' (*Ballad of the Mari Lwyd*) and went on to elaborate in his 'Music of Colours' poems, perhaps most importantly in 'Music of Colours, White Blossom', from *The Lady with the Unicorn*. This collection has always seemed to me the first of the mature Watkins. Not only is the title-poem his most explicit statement of the power of art over time, but also that human love, which inspired the making of the tapestries he describes and celebrates, is akin to divine love, sacred in its own right and a powerful force in the destruction of the idea of time. The book opens with the marvellous introductory poem, 'Music of Colours, White

Blossom', first of a series with related titles, and one essential to the understanding of Watkins's thought. In this he makes plain his idea that for any revelation—any true revelation—of the eternal world, Christ's intervention, presence even, is necessary. The genesis of the poem, he wrote, 'was suggested in winter by a fall of snow on the sea cliff . . . I walked out on the cliff and found that the foam of the sea, which had been brilliantly white the previous day, now looked grey'.[7] Seeing this, Watkins realises that the only real whiteness 'must have been/ When His eyes looked down and made the leper clean'. The true colours of the eternal world are visible only in the perfect white of Christ.

The poem is written in irregular verse-paragraphs; some have seven lines, some six, some five and some three. The rhyming is also irregular, but the rhythm is firmly iambic, some lines being octosyllabic while most are pentameters. It opens with a splendid celebration of the one colour without which no other colour is possible; it is like a celebration of elemental truth:

> *White blossom, white, white shell; the Nazarene*
> *Walking in the ear; white touched by souls*
> *Who know the music by which white is seen,*
> *Blinding white, from strings and aureoles,*
> *Until that is not white, seen at the two poles,*
> *Nor white the Scythian hills, nor Marlowe's queen.*

This is quite clearly the result of his cliff-top walk. Marvellously white though it seems, the new snow—even that seen 'at the two poles'—is not white compared with the 'blinding white' known as a result of a vision of Christ's world; nor, indeed, is blossom, nor shell, nor any image from our mortal world. The development of the poem, through the statement of the spray which 'looked white until this snowfall' and the firm certainty of 'call nothing white again', leads him to the conclusion that in all the world of nature, beautiful though it is, there is no true white. Nor is everybody aware of 'blinding white' even when close to Christ:

> *If there is white, or has been white, it must have been*
> *When His eyes looked down and made the leper clean.*
> *White will not be, apart, though the trees try*
> *Spirals of blossom, their green conspiracy.*
> *She who touched His garment saw no white tree.*

From the natural world the poem moves into a stanza in praise of the glorious examples of whiteness to be found in myth. The curious juxtaposition of Christian and pagan imagery, reminiscent of Renaissance poetry in this at least, is really perfectly logical. (Watkins was intensely interested in myth as a kind of genuine but faulty recognition of truth, a kind of pre-Christian, half-knowledgeable religion. It is partly this which makes the poetry of Hölderlin, combining as it does Christian and Greek belief, so attractive to him.) Having been made aware of perfect whiteness, Watkins is all the more able to recognise and appreciate the less perfect:

> *Lovers speak of Venus, and the white doves,*
> *Jubilant, the white girl, myth's whiteness, Jove's,*
> *Of Leda, the swan, whitest of his loves . . .*

but he knows, too, that:

> *I know nothing of Earth or colour until I know I lack*
> *Original white . . .*

It is this knowledge that marks his verse. True inspiration, argues Watkins, is that knowledge of the perfect and time-less world which Christ allows, briefly and occasionally, to the true artist. It is the task of the artist to see that eternity clear when the vision is offered to him, in a flash of 'blinding white', and to recreate it as humbly and as perfectly as possible for his fellow-men through the practice of his art.

But this is an enormously important responsibility, the greatest a man can assume. We can guess that Watkins, a modest man, might have been wary of making so great a claim for his own art, and this might account for the many poems in which other artists are mentioned, and for those poems in which poets are urged to caution:

> *Poets, in whom truth lives*
> *Until you say you know . . .*

For that is the danger. Poets do *not* know: they are *told*, if they wait humbly and patiently and are strong in their faith:

> *Strong is your trust; then wait:*
> *Your King comes late.*
> ('Poet's in Whom Truth Lives')

Watkins's position at this time must have troubled him deeply. For so modest a man to discuss the nature of inspiration directly and personally would·have been unthinkable, yet it is obvious from poems in *The Death Bell* and *Cypress and Acacia* that these are the concerns that obsessed him. His solution was beautifully simple and successful. He assumed a mask, a persona which allowed him to speak in the first person; not as Vernon Watkins the twentieth century bank clerk, but as Taliesin the sixth- century poet.

Why Taliesin should so have attracted Watkins is fairly obvious, for Taliesin in his *Hanes Taliesin* claims to be quite out of the sway of time. He has witnessed events thousands of years apart:

> *I was nearly nine months in the belly of the hag Caridwen*
> *I was first Little Gwion, at length I am Taliesin.*
> *I was with my Lord in the highest sphere*

When Lucifer fell into the depths of Hell.
I carried the banner before Alexander.
I know the names of the stars from the North to the
South . . .
I was the chief overseer at the building of the tower of
Nimrod
I was on the high cross of the merciful Son of God . . . [8]

It was this prophetic power of poetry in which all time, past, present and future, remained as one that so attracted Watkins. He identified himself with the old poet, he laid claim to him. His first such poem was 'Taliesin in Gower', in which Watkins walks, as Taliesin, over his own Gower cliffs:

Late I return, O violent, colossal, reverberant,
eavesdropping sea.
My country is here. I am foal and violet. Hawthorn breaks
from my hands . . .

(It is worth pointing out here that foal, violet and hawthorn are all symbols of regenerative life in Watkins's work, all stand for the defeat of time and can be met in many poems.)

But the important Taliesin poem is 'Taliesin and the Spring of Vision'; important for my argument that is. For Taliesin in the Mabinogion story had, as a child, drunk the three magic drops of inspiration that splashed onto his finger from the Cauldron of Knowledge, and all time was revealed to him. Now Watkins can look at the nature of inspiration, can make all his great claims, not on his own behalf but on behalf of all true poets, through the mouth of Taliesin. He can examine his own position and the modifications he may wish to make in his idea of the nature of inspiration, time, religion. For Taliesin is the witness at once of present, future and past; in his presence, we learn, 'time's glass breaks'. But Watkins/Taliesin is not ready for such knowledge:

> So sang the grains of sand,. and while they whirled
>   to a pattern·
> Taliesin took refuge under the unfledged rock.
> He could not see in the cave, but groped with his hands,
> And the rock he touched was the socket of all men's eyes,
> And he touched the spring of vision . . .

This is a remarkable and precise description of a mystical experience. If it is not as matter-of-fact and concrete as the parallel description of Gwion's revelation, (Gwion was the boy who became Taliesin, and who swallowed the magic drops), we may assume that this is because Watkins is writing of his own experience. The real Taliesin seems never to have had any doubt, he exulted in his all-embracing knowledge and his free progress in one guise or another backwards and forwards through time:

> Primary chief bard am I to Elphin,
> And my original country is the region of the summer stars;
> Idno and Heino called me Merddin,
> At length every king will call me Taliesin . . . '[9]

But complete and total vision of this sort is too great for Watkins, although he is to experience it for a moment:

> And he touched the spring of vision. He had the mind
>   of a fish[10]
> That moment. He knew the glitter of scale and fin.
> He touched the pin of pivotal space, and saw
> One sandgrain balance the ages' cumulus cloud.

Such knowledge is too heavy for frail humanity:
> Earth's shadow hung. Taliesin said: 'The penumbra of
>   history is terrible.
> Life changes, breaks, scatters, there is no sheet-anchor . . .

Most terrible of all for Watkins:
>   Time reigns . . .

This, a despairing admission for the poet, yet is no more than the recognition that time's rule is tenuous and easily conquerable. Human love can defeat time by its intensity and devotion and most markedly through works of art ('inward acts, acts corresponding to music'); divine love is so perfect that time does not exist in its presence:

> *Time reigns; yet the kingdom of love is every moment,*
> *Whose citizens do not age in each other's eyes.*
> *In a time of darkness the pattern of life is restored*
> *By men who make all transience seem an illusion*
> *Through inward acts, acts corresponding to music*
> *Their works of love leave words that do not end in the heart.*

We are prepared for this, knowing that 'poets in whom truth lives' can 'by acts corresponding to music' make 'all transience seem an illusion'.

But there is further revelation. Taliesin has not yet relinquished his vision:

> *He still held rock. Then three drops fell on his fingers,*
> *And Future and Past converged in a lightning flash:*

This is the true knowledge. These are the three 'drops of the charmed liquor' that fell from the Cauldron of Inspiration. They speak to Watkins, in his Taliesin robes:

> *It was we who instructed Shakespeare, who fell upon Dante's*
> *eyes,*
> *Who opened to Blake the Minute Particulars. We are the*
> *soul's rebirth.*

And we understand that true poetic knowledge — for Shakespeare, Blake and Dante are three of Watkins's heroes, and two at least have revealed a knowledge of Heaven and Hell as profound as Taliesin's—is equivalent to the soul's rebirth. This is what inspiration means. But nobody can live at this pitch continually:

Taliesin answered: 'I have encountered the irreducible diamond
In the rock. Yet now it is over. Omniscience is not for man.
Christen me, therefore, that my acts in the dark may be just,
And adapt my partial vision to the limitation of time.'

For our modern Taliesin cannot hold forever 'the irreducible diamond in the rock', the absolute knowledge that he gained momentarily. 'Human kind,' writes Eliot, 'cannot bear very much reality', and Watkins repeats that 'omniscience is not for man'. He knows that his day-to-day life is all too human, all too subject to the dictates of man-invented time. In uninspired days he will not see clearly and it is only through Christ that his 'partial vision' will be adapted 'to the limitation of Time'.

'Taliesin and the Spring of Vision' is included in *Cypress and Acacia*, a volume in which Watkins, as I have suggested, has been concerned to examine the nature of inspiration and, if I am right, to state publicly his assumption of the poet's heroic responsibility, that of seeing and interpreting Eternity. To complete his task he must have read very widely the work of other poets and considered the work of artists in other media. My belief is that, in *Cypress and Acacia*, Watkins marshalled all the support he could. My first hint of this – outside the identification with Taliesin – is to be found in the charming poem, 'The Mare'. Stephen Spender's poem,[11] more famous, perhaps, thirty years ago than it is today, has these lines:

Eye, gazelle, delicate wanderer,
Drinker of the horizon's fluid line . . .
                              (Not palaces, an era's crown . . .)

The mare lies down in the grass where the nest of the skylark
  is hidden
Her eyes drink the delicate horizon moving behind the
  song . . .

It is as if Watkins is reminding us of the examples of truth he finds in other poets: for this is only one of a number of passages in which he recalls the work of other men, sometimes, as here, in the borrowing of a simple image, sometimes by writing a whole poem in a manner that irresistibly recalls another poet. It is as if, having made his enormous claims for the importance, the necessity, of the poet's task, he is claiming support of his peers, he is 'numbering them in the song'. He has already called on Taliesin, Shakespeare, Blake, Dante, Spender, but they are only the first in a long line of poets named or remembered in this extraordinary volume; sometimes, as in 'The Mare', by specific use of unmistakable lines or images, sometimes, as in 'The Return', by the use of forms and titles which recall those used by other poets; and sometimes, as in 'A Wreath for Alun Lewis' and 'In the Protestant Cemetary, Rome', by writing his elegies for the young poets whose moments of truth were curtailed by death.

It cannot be the purpose of this essay to examine all these correspondences in complete detail, but readers may find it interesting to compare 'Christ and Charon' with F.T.Prince's remarkable poem 'Campanella'. [12] The two poems are very alike in movement, both using a sonorous and flexible iambic measure; and in theme, the evocation of a free world of brotherhood imagined from a scene of unrelieved horror. Watkins writes from the banks of the Styx, Prince's historical Campanella argues his passionate certainties from the torture-chamber. But any comparison of the two poems will reveal a similarity of vocabulary and imagery which is surprising. Both men dream of a world of 'brotherhood': in Watkins's poem, Charon is accompanied by '*vultures* past redemption' and Prince's hero is tortured by 'tyrants, *vultures*, hypocrites' - and these are also 'past redemption'. These are only a few of many similarities. Again, in 'The Return' Watkins gives us his intention in the title, so reminiscent of those used by Henry Vaughan, the poet with whom Watkins had much else in common. He then confirms our presumption by using a verse-form very like those of Vaughan, although he was such a consummate craftsman that he was able to invent one in the old Silurist's manner rather than adopt one already used. In this interesting experiment, Watkins adopts a seventeenth-century manner, and almost a seventeenth-century language, to deal with a traditional theme; the return of a disturbing ghost. But the ghost returns in a decidedly contemporary way:

> *I lay, pulse beating fast,*
> *While the night raider passed*
> *And gave each hovering tick*
> *The speed of dream.*
> *Sleep in the dead of night could make all quick,*
> *Reverse the extreme*
> *Outrider's task on thought's magnetic beam.*

Here, it seems to me, the poet's admiration for Vaughan is evident, and he has called on the Breconshire poet for his aid.

Similarly, perhaps even more obviously, we find the voice of Tennyson in 'Camelot'. Again the title is evocative and we are unlikely to miss the allusion. Watkins was, in any event, widely read in the Romantic poets, and he was able to work very successfully in a recognisable area of Tennyson's material as well as in his style:

> She that was a queen stood here
> Where the kestrel hovers.
> He was resting by the weir:
> He and she were lovers.
> Praise and passion in her throat
> Breathed above her psalter
> Long before King Arthur's boat
> Moved upon the water.

Other correspondences are not hard to find. 'The Curlew' calls upon Yeats, on Tennyson, very clearly on Keats, particularly in the lines:

> Sweet-throated cry, by one no longer heard
> Who, more than many, loved the wandering bird,
> Unchanged through generations and renewed . . .

Surely we are asked to recall:

> Thou wast not born for death, immortal Bird:
> No hungry generations tread thee down . . .

Watkins himself tells us in 'Touch with Your Fingers'— a poem written rather in the style of de la Mare — that his celebration of other poets is deliberate and conscious:

> What then compelled me
> To take on trust
> Words of the poets
> Laid in dust?
> Time cannot answer.
> True love must.

And those six lines are almost a summary and justification of my thesis.

We have seen that Watkins takes 'on trust' the work of poets widely separated in time and language, and perhaps we need only two more examples to indicate the depth and the systematic thoroughness of Watkins's concern with the responsibility of true poets and his examination of the way in which other men had accepted that responsibility. The first is Wilfred Owen, for whose poetry Watkins had a great admiration. 'Angel and Man', a long conversation poem, bears all the marks of deliberate tribute; its assonances (miracles/oracles; dawn/down; fall/feel; ever/over) are often those used by Owen himself, its diction irresistibly recalls some of Owen's work, and, in particular, 'Strange Meeting';

> *Faint incarnation in the mists of dawn,*
> *Why do you rouse desires I have laid down*
> *On this sad field where the world tends her wounded* . . .

And again:

> . . . *Grief was theirs,*
> *And grief, their lot, is likely to be mine.*

which is bound to remind us of:

> *Courage was mine, and I had mystery,*
> *Wisdom was mine, and I had mystery* . . .

All this is an achievement of a most rare kind. For despite these deliberate references to the work of other poets, Watkins retained his markedly individual voice. His exploration into the nature of poetry remained a personal journey, his assumption of poetic responsibility, despite the examples he displays to us, is clearly his own realisation. Even his interest in old Welsh poetry, of which his 'Taliesen' poems are evidence, is used to further his purpose. Some of the rhymes in 'Angel and Man', for example, may remind us of the rhyming of stressed and unstressed syllables we find in the *cywydd*. This is not an easy form to sustain in English, but Watkins attempts it in rhymes such as 'field/fulfilled' and 'lived/deceived'. Clearer evidence, though, is to be found in 'The Tributary Seasons'. Here he used one of the most famous images in Welsh poetry, taken from a Llywarch Hen poem. That he knew these poems is shown by Glyn Jones, who writes:

> With Dr. T.J. Morgan I had at that time just published a translation and reconstruction of some old Welsh poetry, the ninth-century Llywarch Hen poems. Vernon knew about the book and told me that his father had been keenly interested in this poetry, in Aneirin, Taliesin and Llywarch Hen, and used to read English translations of it to him when he was a child . . . [14]

Watkins begins 'The Tributary Seasons' with these lines:

> *I can discern at last how grew*
> *This tree, so naked and so true.*
> *'Spring was my death; when all is sung,*
> *It was the Autumn made me young.'*

This seems to have been suggested by the lines from Llywarch Hen:

> *This leaf the wind whirls about,*
> *Alas for its fate —*
> *Born this year, old already* . . . [15]

It seems likely, too, that Watkins knew the anonymous tenth-century Welsh poem, 'Winter'; for after his image of the 'autumn-born' tree, he continues:

> *Midwinter; packed with ice the butt,*
> *Splitting its sides.*
> *Roots hard as iron; the back door shut* . . .

While the Welsh poem begins:

Wind is sharp, hillside bleak, hard to win shelter;
Ford is impassable, lake is frozen;
A man may stand on one blade of grass.[16]

Accepting, then, that Watkins, in *Cypress and Acacia*, was proving the necessity of true art, explaining to us the purpose of the true poet, we can find additional significance in the three elegies for young poets which are included in the collection; 'In the Protestant Cemetery, Rome', in which Watkins, recalling his first visit to the graves of Keats, Shelley and Trelawney in that spot 'where cypress and acacia stand', tells us that it was a time of deep personal trouble, a moment 'when I still/ Knew no remedy for time's ill'; 'A wreath for Alun Lewis', his lament for one who is 'needed now, for you knew men's strength and failing,/ Their death by storm who could manage intricate chords . . . '; and 'The Exacting Ghost', a splendid elegy for, as I take it, Dylan Thomas. This last is a fine poem, moving with a simple solemnity that I find very impressive. Nowhere strained or unsteady, its calm surface reveals a profound and unrelieved sadness over the death of his friend, and it achieves a direct, uncomplicated statement which is almost new in Watkins's verse, although it is to appear more and more frequently in subsequent poems:

Last night, when sleep had given back the power
To see what nature had withdrawn,
I saw corrected by that hour,
All likenesses the mind had drawn.

In crowded tavern you I found
Conversing there, yet knew you dead.
This was no ghost. When you turned round,
It was indeed your living head.

Time had returned . . .

But I fear that I have already unbalanced the argument of this essay with too many examples. An interested reader can trace for himself the importance of poems like 'Poet and Goldsmith', 'A Man with a Field', and others, to my general theme, and consider whether these poems may not be best thought of as one single work almost, so closely related are they to Watkins's great obsessions.

And his giant purpose is continued, modified and expanded in *Affinities,* the collection published in 1962 when Watkins was fifty-six years old. 'In this book Vernon Watkins is ploughing old ground'[17] said the poet wryly, when his publisher asked him for a blurb for the book. It has a certain truth: many of the poems are written on themes he has examined before, and some rely for a full understanding on a knowledge of these earlier poems. His statement implies, too, that it is a collection of considered work, that the excitement of discovery may well be missing. And it is true that the exploration of the nature of poetry and inspiration which resulted in the Taliesin poems among others is here only as a statement of belief. There is an extension of his interest to true interpreters in other arts; Michaelangelo and Nijinsky are celebrated. There is an important dialogue conducted between the poet and his muse in 'Demands of the Poet' and 'Demands of the Muse', in which Watkins states the essential labour ('I set my heart against all lesser toil') and continuous struggle of the true poet ('It is by conflict that he knows me And serves me in my way and not another'). As in *Cypress and Acacia,* true poets are invoked and honoured, among them Thomas ('A True Picture Restored'), Lawrence ('Zennor Cottages'), Wordsworth, Eliot, Keats, Charles Williams, Heine, Browning and Hölderlin. There are, in addition, two 'Taliesin' poems which keep the great theme before us.

The Browning poem, 'Browning in Venice', is a particularly interesting example of Watkins's uncommon skill.

Kathleen Raine has told us that:

It was like him, too, to have gone to so much trouble, in Venice, to get the key to Browning's Palazzo, which he visited in the spirit of pilgrimage.[18]

And it is in the 'spirit of pilgrimage' that all the poems in the section beginning with 'Héloise' and ending with 'Browning in Venice' are written. In one sense, indeed, all the poems in this book are written in such a spirit. Certainly the Browning poem is whole-hearted in its admiration. We have seen that Watkins possessed so marked a sense of style that he could, very successfully, use a manner clearly reminiscent of the poet he was discussing without ever losing his own voice, and in this poem he invents a stanza form so markedly Browningesque that I searched the *Collected Poems* for the model; but Browning has used no form exactly like the one Watkins has 'forged'—a necessary pun— for him. The ten-line stanza, using lines of varying but strictly-controlled lengths and a complex rhyme scheme, often give us an eerie echo of Browning's voice. The nearest examples of similar forms I can find in Browning are those used in 'Love Among the Ruins' and 'The Grammarian's Funeral' and it is interesting to compare the three poems. Again, as in the Keats sonnet in this same collection ('The Death of Keats'), Watkins is at pains to claim, not the individual achievement of any one poet, but the primary affinity of true poetry:

The achievement does not matter, nor the fame;

and in this his purpose is not unlike that he examined and displayed in *Cypress and Acacia*. But the heart of this more recent collection is his absorption with the poetry of Hölderlin, and 'The Childhood of Hölderlin' occupies the central section of the book. This long poem, written in nine parts is prefaced by Watkins's own translation of Hölderlin's 'To the Fates', (An Die Parzen). Watkins had admired Michael Hamburger's translation of this famous poem,[19] and its importance to his own preoccupations at this time is obvious. It is a statement absolutely in accord with his own belief that the poet's gift was a 'god-like right', and that having once composed his 'full-ripened songs' he has lived 'as gods live'. It is not the sort of completely romantic statement that Watkins could make in his own person or claim directly for himself, but he has been in effect making such a claim on behalf of all the artists he has been celebrating. Now, in the first person, even if momentarily speaking as Hölderlin, he can make his eloquent boast of the heightened, indeed 'god-like' perceptions of the poet, make open the peculiar satisfactions they bring and the risks that are attendant:

> *Only one Summer grant, you Powerful Ones,*
> *And one Autumn to my full-ripened song,*
> *That my heart willingly by the tender*
> *Harp-strings be satisfied; let me die, then.*
>
> *The soul to which its god-like right when alive*
> *Came not, down in Orcus shall find no rest;*
> *But once the holy one that against*
> *My heart, the poem, is uttered,*
>
> *Welcome, then, O peace of the world of Shades!*
> *Content am I, even if the play of strings*
> *Has not down-guided my footsteps; once*
> *Lived I as gods live, and more I crave not.*

It is the sort of high gesture not really open to a contemporary poet, but essentially it is what Watkins had been wanting to say for some time.

For a full understanding of the long 'The Childhood of Hölderlin' some knowledge of the German poet's life and work is necessary; without them the poem is certainly the reflection of Watkins's excited recognition of his own central beliefs vividly anticipated by the older poet, but it could also be an obscure work. It is probably enough here to say that Hölderlin shared Watkins's interest in the inter-relationship of pagan and Christian belief, that his attempts to integrate Greek myth and Christianity must have been most helpful and encouraging to Watkins, and that his opinion of the high and necessary nature of the poet's task was identical with that of Watkins.

Beginning, then, with his first true poems, Watkins's work had been a long revelation of eternity as he was allowed to see it; he had searched for the example, the support and assurance of other true artists, finding his greatest help in the work of the old Welsh poet Taliesin and that of the modern German poet Hölderlin. His own world, compounded now of what he saw about him with his ordinary eyes and what he knew of the eternal world, was ready for exploration. In the beautiful poem 'Waterfalls', the first in *Affinities,* we see Watkins treat, almost for the first time, the natural world about him with the intensity he had reserved for the immortal world. In 'Poem for Conrad' there is a beautifully exact and humorous observation at work to create an extension of his sensibility that I, for one, had not thought possible. In 'The Guest', a miraculous poem from *Fidelities*, he makes our mortal world eternal, and proves his claim for art's defeat of time through lines which are so perfect that they seem without art. I am still surprised by the lovely combination of visual and aural imagery in this stanza from 'The Guest', by the sensuous precision and clarity which allows us to see and to hear the thrush crack his snail's shell in the last line:

The cliff's crossed path lay silvered with slug tracks
Where webs of hanging raindrops caught the sun.

A thrush with snail cocked sideways like an axe
Knocked with quick beak to crack it on a stone . . .

Nor can I forget, in the same poem, this unusual precision of observed and realised detail:

Stumbling, a blue-black beetle groped its way
Where crickets perched and dropped like jewelry . . .

Or:

There, halfway down the cliff, in fallen flight
I came on plumage, tufted claws, wide wings,
A white owl dead, feeding fritillary light
Into those roots from which the heather springs.

And there are other examples in his last work. He had achieved the synthesis of the mortal and eternal worlds, alas almost too late.

  For he was a very rare type of poet indeed, one who spent most of his life to make with infinite labour the groundwork of an enormous edifice, his ambitious plans embracing the deepest mysteries of life and art. He was wholly serious and dedicated; his concerns were those of absolute great poetry. Whatever his stature, and we are too near to him in time to discuss this, his work is certainly unique in our generation.

Notes
1. From 'Poets on Poetry', a series under that title contributed to the literary magazine *x*. Watkins's aphorisms appeared in *x*, 1, 2 (March 1960), pp.153–154.
2. ibid.
3. Particularly in her book *Defending Ancient Springs*; but see also *Vernon Watkins 1906-1967*, (Faber and Faber).
4. In *Triskel One.*
5. Quoted by Gwen Watkins in *Vernon Watkins 1906- 1967*

6. St. Luke, chapter 19, verses 2-3.
7. Vernon Watkins, *Poetry and Experience*.
8. Trans. D.W.Nash.
9. *The Mabinogion*, trans. Lady Charlotte Guest.
10. This powerfully evocative image suggests that Taliesin not only had knowledge of pre-historic events, but of pre-natal existence. Watkins has taken it from *Hanes Taliesin:*

> *I am able to instruct the whole universe.*
> *I shall be until the day of doom on the face of the earth;*
> *And it is not known whether my body is flesh or fish.*
>
> *(The Mabinogion).*

11. Stephen Spender, *Poems*, (Faber and Faber) 1933, p. 56.
12. F.T.Prince, *The Doors of Stone*, (Rupert Hart-Davis), p. 112.
13. It is unnecessary to say that

> *I saw Eternity the other night*
> *Like a great* Ring *of pure and endless light* . . .

might be the lines for which Watkins constantly strove; but there are many resemblances. Both Vaughan and Watkins are Welshmen writing in English, both are symbolic poets for whom 'white' and 'light' are of central importance, both are concerned with the recognition of the immortal world and the necessary defeat of time.
14. Glyn Jones, in *Vernon Watkins 1906-1967*.
15. From *The Saga of Llywarch the Old*, trans. Glyn Jones and T.J. Morgan (Golden Cockerel Press 1955)
16. *The Penguin Book of Welsh Verse*, trans. A.Conran (Penguin 1967).
This is not, of course, the translation Watkins would have known.
17. Quoted by Gwen Watkins in *Vernon Watkins 1906-1967* p. 18.
18. Kathleen Raine, ibid.
19. The relationship between Watkins's work and

Hölderlin's really needs an essay to itself. Apart from the obvious fact that many poets of Watkins's generation turned naturally to Hölderlin, because in Spender's words, the modern poet finds 'again and again that this strange poetry which combines nostalgia and prophecy and disintegration with a passionate desire for fusion expresses situations which recur in his own experience of the apocalyptic times in which we live', (*The Listener*, Vol. 36, No. 918, 1946), but the German poet anticipated *exactly* many of Watkins's own conclusions. In addition to those I mention, too cursorily, in this essay, both poets thought, for example, that children were possessed of unusual qualities, perhaps superhuman qualities. Central to our understanding of this relationship is a study of *Poems of Hölderlin*, trans. by Michael Hamburger, (Nicholson and Watson, 1943). Hamburger, a friend of long standing, sent Watkins a copy of the book when it appeared.

PENNAR DAVIES

PENNAR DAVIES: MORE THAN A POETA DOCTUS

J. Gwyn Griffiths

It is an apt moment to consider the poetry of Pennar Davies since has recently published a new volume of verse, *Y Tlws yn y Lotws* (The Jewel in the Lotus). This is his sixth collection of poems. The following are the details:

(1) Seven poems in *Modern Welsh Poetry*, ed. Keidrych Rhys (London, 1944), pp. 13-17.

(2) *Cinio'r Cythraul*. 35 pp. (Denbigh, 1946)

(3) *Cerddi Cadwgan*. pp. 13-30. (Swansea, 1953) His is the longest of the five contributions.

(4) *Naw Wfft*. 44 pp. (Denbigh, 1957)

(5) *Yr Efrydd o Lyn Cynon*. 60 pp. (Llandybie, 1961)

(6) *Y Tlws yn y Lotws*. 76 pp. (Llandybie, 1971)

The first two were published under the name of Davies Aberpennar. William Thomas Davies is the poet's name as determined by his parents. He has adopted the additional *praenomen* Pennar because he was born in Aberpennar (Mountain Ash).

It may be noted that the early titles *Cinio'r Cythraul* (The Devil's Dinner) and *Naw Wfft* (An Ennead of Damns) have a much more rebellious aura than *Yr Efrydd o Lyn Cynon* (The Cripple from Glyn Cynon) or the new lotus-offering. One might be tempted to think that this is a sign of softening, something that comes inevitably with mellowness and maturity. This would be quite wrong. The rebellion is still there, although there are a few touches of resignation in the new book, as when the poet ends his longish piece about Ulysses with the comforting thought that, as with Telemachus, so the final battle will be fought by his son.

English is the language of the earliest group of poems although their themes are intensely Welsh. To him Welsh was an acquired language and the reasons for his eventual decision to use Welsh in his writing are vigorously set out in the chapter he has contributed to *Artists in Wales* (ed. Meic Stephens, Llandysul, 1971). It was an act of deliberate commitment. In his brief introductory note Mr. Stephens refers to some of the other works of Pennar Davies. They include novels, a volume of short stories, works on church history, a bibliography of John Bale published by the Oxford University Press, an exciting book on early Welsh mythology and religion, *Rhwng Chwedl a Chredo* (Between Myth and Creed), and a *journal intime* of great charm, *Cudd fy Meiau* (Hide My Sins). Mr. Stephens, by the way, lists the last-named work as a novel. I dare say he has every right to do so. Today almost anything can go by that name or as an anti-novel. The author's sub-title is *Dyddlyfr y Brawd o Radd Isel* (The Diary of the Brother of Low Degree). I shall not attempt here to relate this many-sided and exuberant literary activity to the poetry, except to note that the poetic treatment of the Arthurian legend is illuminated by the admirable discussion of the theme in *Rhwng Chwedl a Chredo*.

Although the contributions to *Modern Welsh Poetry* are untypical in their medium, they share one quality with much of the subsequent work in Welsh. This is their wide-ranging allusiveness. There is a good example (indeed several) in his 'Poem for D. Robert Griffiths', an elegy whose stanzas are interlaced with lines by D. R. Griffiths parodying the style of some Anglo-Welsh writers, as for instance:

*Tomos Tin Whistle don't sing Comfort Ye like old Jenkins
the Gin do 'e?
No mun old Tomos do only see the lines but Jenkins the Gin*

did sing wot was between the lines too mun.

The opening elegiac couplet reads thus:

> *Strew on her bloaters, bloaters — for her God
> Won't mind at all — but not a bone of cod.*

Bloaters are aptly chosen for the late lamented lady since we
are told later that

> *Salt is the sea, and salt the tears we shed.
> Will you have fish and chips or laver-bread?*

Salt is the sea, and salt the tears we shed.
Will you have fish and chips or laver-bread?
There was a mournful ditty current in the valleys of
Southern Wales, sung to *Tôn y Botel:*
*Who stole a bloater (ter)
From Mrs. Thomas the Fat?*

If there is an echo, perhaps, of this plebeian dirge, the form
of the opening couplet follows of course Matthew Arnold's
'Requiescat'.

> *Strew on her roses, roses
> And never a spray of yew.*

It is the closing couplet, however, that provides the poem's
most memorable picture:

> *Behold the Fish of God that takes away
> The stinks of all the world, now and for aye.*

One reviewer raised eyebrows at the hint of blasphemy which he thought was here bringing a sea-change to the Lamb of God. The Fish, however, was a sacred symbol of the early Christians. 'Jesus Christ, Son of God, Saviour' were the words which they cryptically associated with ICHTHUS, the Greek word for fish, because the letters are the initial letters of the words in the Greek title. Here, then, is a felicitous application of the ancient symbol to a modern context.

A plethora of allusions may be found in any of the six collections, and *Y Tlws yn y Lotws* teems with them. The lotus itself is the central symbol of two of the poems here; it derives from Tibetan Buddhism, which sees the pearl in the lotus as the cosmic fulfilment of life and love; it has nothing to do with the sleepy *Lotophagoi* of Homer or the young sun-god Nefertem arising from the lotus in the Egyptian tradition in which Tutankhamun is figured. But the type of allusiveness which concerns me now is more peripheral. 'Celein Veinwen' is a nostalgic poem about the death of an Aber-pennar boy from diphtheria; after suggesting the strange charm of the corpse (*Rhosyn gwyn ydoedd yn ei arch*, he was a white rose in his coffin) the poet points to the resignation they could not avoid:

> *Nid oedd dim byd i'w wneud ond derbyn*
> *absenoldeb yr hen grwt annwyl,*
> *presenoldeb y Pantocrator.*

(There was nothing to do but accept the absence of the dear darling boy, the presence of the Pantocrator).

This poem, incidentally, is stylistically spare and limpid when compared with the lush and viscous richness of the idiom mostly used in the volume. The Pantocrator is Christ the All-ruler, a figure familiar in Byzantine and other early Christian art; in the Apocalypse it is the culminating term in describing Christ who is Alpha and Omega, the beginning and end. It is out of place, one might think, in the account of the family's reaction to Arthur's death. Still, the poet is telling the tale, and he is entitled to use the image which appeals to him. Certainly it impresses in its swift summation.

Again, in 'Y Lloer' he laments the passing of the romantic kingdom associated with the moon. The conquest of the moon by astronaut-*homunculi* has buried the old domain of romance:

> *y deyrnas goll i gyd yn gaeth*
> *o dan arglwyddiaeth*
> *brenhines y sêr penysgeifn*
> *yn ei llong arian ar gefnfor glas nen y nos,*
> *Selene, Messiatz, Heng-ngo, Arianrhod.*

(the lost kingdom all enslaved under sovereignty of the queen of the carefree stars in her silver ship on the blue deep of the night sky, Selene, Messiatz, Heng-ngo, Arianrhod).

The last line lists moon-goddesses — Greek, Slavonic, Chinese, Early Welsh ('Silver Wheel', if that is the meaning, recalls 'silver ship'). Arianrhod is connected by some with the Corona Borealis rather than the moon. Messiatz is not easy to track down. The form is a bit like Metztli, the Aztec moon god (and Pennar Davies is well versed in everything Aztec), but my wife reminds me that *Messiatz* is pretty close to the Russian word for moon, and indeed G.Alexinsky in Larousse *Encyclopedia of Mythology*, in an *exposé* of myths, tells us that 'though the name of the Moon—Myesyats — is masculine, many legends represent Myesyats as a young beauty whom the Sun marries at the beginning of summer, abandons in winter, and returns to in spring.' The moon 'in her silver ship' is an instructive image; the Greeks used to envisage her in a chariot, but the Egyptians imagined both sun and moon as voyaging in ships, a point noted by Plutarch in ch.34 of his book on Isis and Osiris.

Is the poet open to the charge of pursuing an ostentatious Alexandrinism? His allusions, it may be claimed, are an integral part of his presentation, even if they sometimes seem to be recondite and *recherché*. The rich deployment of Welsh lore and myth is refreshingly accompanied by evocations of many other cultures. As the poet aptly says himself (*Artists in Wales,* 125), 'to accept the vocation of the Welsh artist is not, of course, to part company with the world.' He notes that when he published, in Welsh, stories about a Spanish nun and a Soviet scientist (not in conjunction, one should add), 'no one suggested that I was the less Welsh for doing so.' Yet there is a touch of injured self-defence when he goes on like this:

> 'Parochialism is of the mind; the Welsh language is of Europe and of the world. Not that all Welsh readers are prepared to accept this. I have frequently been accused, at least by implication, of something like polymathic exhibitionism because I have not hesitated to share my reading with my readers.

The truth is that there has been also a measure of positive and appreciative reaction, and he himself is able to add that, in his view, 'the consumers of Welsh literature are beginning to tolerate unfamiliar allusions, recondite ideas and subtleties of expression.'

Furthermore, this poetry may sometimes prove difficult, but it is never obscure. Often it involves, through allusion, the presentation of the visual and concrete which is at the heart of poetry. Thus in a poem 'To the Night' the idea of inscrutable mystery is conveyed in a swift double invocation of Roman and Welsh mythology:

Tyrd, Nos, y nwydwyllt Nos, tyrd, Nos, a dywed
Sut treisiodd Tarcwin y ddi-nam Lwcrês,
Sut collodd plas Cynddylan hoen a gwres —
Ti wyddost, noethlom Nos. Gad inni glywed.

(Come, Night, wildly passionate Night, come, Night and tell how Tarquin raped the blameless Lucretia, how the hall of Cynddylan lost ecstasy and warmth. You know, naked-arid Night. Let us hear).

To Pennar Davies literature can be a vital source of inspiration. His poem 'Pedair Diweddeb' ('Four Endings')— really a group of four poems is a striking instance. He has taken the title from musical terminology, following the types of final chords, and with these he links parts of the four quotations which, he tells us in a footnote, have provided the initial impetus of the poems. In addition he addresses each poem to a real person, so that the four subtitles have each three elements, thus (in translation):

I. E COME FANTOLIN: A PERFECT ENDING. To May

Davies

II. GAN D'OLYGON: AN IMPERFECT ENDING. To the

'Grey Lizard, a maid once loved by the poet.

III. MANIBUS DATE: AN UNEXPECTED ENDING. In

memory: Yvette Cauchon.

IV. POURQUOI DONC PENSONS-NOUS: A CHURCH

ENDING. To Rosemarie Wolff.

There is a neat *double entendre* in the fourth subtitle, for it was Rosemarie Wolff whom the poet eventually took to the altar. The first quotation is from Dante's *Paradiso* and concerns the love shown to Mary by the saints; it is like that of the infant who raises his arms to his mother after taking her milk. Although the lovely Beatrice is with Dante, this context is far from being erotic. The poet assures his love that he has seen her beauty:

Ond gwelais innau di a thyfais yng nghroth dy gariad.

(But I saw you and grew in the womb of your love).

It seems that the loved one is equated in some way with the Virgin; but the literary and living experiences do not quite merge. Problems of *Dichtung und Wahrheit* are not easy to resolve in a poet whose avowed literary incentives are so assertive.

There is a radiant felicity, on the other hand, in the lines from the Welsh *cywydd* by Dafydd Ionawr which form the centrepiece of the stanzas to the 'Grey Lizard'; and they go well with the poet's own tribute to her. During the confessional sessions of the 'Cadwgan Circle' Pennar used to speak of a ceremonial espousal with the 'Grey Lizard', an Indian girl from Mexico, when he was Commonwealth Fellow at Yale University a little before the Second World War. This was a two-year period, and doubtless much was possible during the long vacations down Mexico way. If the exact truth still evades us, his love for the 'Grey Lizard' (a rendering of her Indian name) is happily immortalised here:

> *Digwyddodd? Darfu? Erys byth*
> *Ein neithior yng nghroniclau'r nef!*
> *Amlinell lom dy angerdd sydd*
> *Fel enfys ar ôl storom gref . . .*

(It happened? It was over? Our wedding feast will ever abide in the records of heaven. The austere outline of your passion is like a rainbow after a mighty storm).

'*Digwyddodd? Darfu?*' echoes the last line of R. Williams Parry's sonnet to the fox. *Manibus date lilia plenis* comes from Vergil's lament for the young Marcellus, and the Welsh poet asks what has become of another maid he had loved, Yvette Cauchon. She is to be found, he says,

Gyda'r Enaid Mawr
A luniodd wallt a chroen a'r byd i gyd.

    (With the Great Soul that made hair and skin and all the world).

The quotation in the last piece is

Pourquoi donc pensons-nous et parlons-nous? C'est drôle;
Nos larmes et nos baisers, eux, ne parlent pas.

With Rosemarie Wolff the poet plans an escape from thoughts and words and a union of kisses and tears. Here the French source and the new experience are seen to be well matched.

    The importance of literature as an impetus is clearly parallel to the fondness for allusion. Life and not literature, one might urge, is the true fount of creative splendour. Where the primal springs flow feebly we find a craving for artifice and pastiche, a general sense of stuffiness. Wilde talked of people whose very passions were but quotations. Is there a danger in yielding to the charms of literature to the extent that they become an initial driving force? The poet, according to Plato, provides us with a copy of a copy; his stricture would apply more sternly still to a poet who contemplated *mimêsis*, in any sense, of poetry already in existence. To this there is a ready riposte if we refuse to regard art as separate and apart from life itself. Literature is an art and as such belongs to the totality of life. A poet has therefore as much right to be influenced by literature as by the other arts such as music and painting; his experience of these things can be as vital as the impress made on him by other living activities. It has been said of W.B. Yeats that he aimed to be a *poeta doctus.* I very much doubt whether Pennar Davies has ever conceived of his poetic mission in this sense. Compared with Yeats he is, of course, a formally equipped scholar in several fields. Yeats had rare gifts and an insatiable intellectual curiosity, but a good deal of his interest in philosophy and oriental thought can be fairly described as the dabbling of a dilletante. Pennar Davies, in contrast, has had the discipline of a long and arduous academic career. Beginning with 'Firsts' in Latin and English in the University of Wales, he proceeded to Balliol College, Oxford, where he took a B.Litt., and then to Yale where he was awarded a doctorate for a study of the comedies of George Chapman. He returned to Oxford, this time to Mansfield College, where he studied theology and Hebrew. Since then he has been mainly involved in the work of the Christian ministry and in academic teaching and research. With such a background a poet might easily cease to be a poet; or he might react strongly, as A.E. Housman did, against the idea that there is any necessary connection between learning and poetry. Pennar Davies has never confused the two. At the same time he clearly believes that poetry involves the whole personality and that it would be disingenuous on his part to write as though a wide expanse of literary achievement in several languages were not familiar to him. I suppose it would be right to describe him as a *poeta doctus.* But he is very much more than that.

For what I have been stressing so far might well obscure the fact that he often has the gift of simple and inspired poetic statement. It is a gift related to his fearless commitment to what he believes in. In 'Golud' ('Riches'), for instance, he tries to persuade his loved one that he is not absolutely destitute:

> *Gwn nad oes gennyf bres na swydd.*
> *Ni allaf ddisgwyl bywyd rhwydd.*
> *Ac eto nid wy'n dlawd.*

Mae gennyf gred, mae gennyf gân,
Ac asbri glew yr Ysbryd Glân,
A'r digywilydd gnawd.

(I know I have no money or post. I cannot expect an easy life. And yet I am not poor. I have a conviction, I have a song, and the daring vivacity of the Holy Spirit, and the unashamed flesh.)

The last couplet may suggest a surprising collocation to which I hope to return presently. In 'Wedi'r Siarad' ('After the Talking') he offers a new version of well-known lines in praise of Wales. Caledfryn is the author of the original *englyn*, which ends thus:

Pa wlad, wedi'r siarad, sydd
Mor lân â Chymru lonydd?

('What land, when all is said, is as fair as tranquil Wales?')

Writing in the context of St David's Day with its orgies of traditional speeches, Pennar Davies is equally lapidary but rather more critical:

'Pa wlad, wedi'r siarad, sydd'
Mor afiach ac mor ufudd?

(What land, when all is said, is so sick and so sycophantic?)

A poem that combines a basic simplicity of style with a wealth of myth and symbol is 'Cathl i'r Almonwydden' ('Song to the Almond Tree'). Its theme is the sheer joy of life, and of resurgent life. Blossoming as it does in mid-winter with an abundant white luxuriance, the almond tree is a Biblical symbol of renewed promise and hope. It guarantees, some months in advance, the coming of spring. The poem begins, however, with a declaration of love of 'many-breasted Nature' *(Natur aml ei bronnau)*, for the poet, like Brendan, has watched her waves; like Elijah he has watched her fire and wind; like Math and Gwydion he has seen the flowers wondrously taking the shape of a drunken Blodeuwedd; with Daphne he has seen the trees becoming

fellow-mourners with the weak and widowed; but he ends
the stanza with praise of the almond tree:

A gwelaf almonwydden
Yn chwifio'i gwynder nwyfus tua'r nen,
Y goeden ddewrwych, hyf, y mwyn, chwerthinog bren.

(And I see an almond tree flaunting her vibrant whiteness
to the heaven, the bravely splendid, audacious tree, the
gentle laughing tree).

The other stanzas have a similar pattern. A wave of joy has
surged over the poet's soul, for he has seen the Lion leaping
over the sun; every sigh has become a paean of praise;
Rachel's tears for her children have become a psalm of
gratitude, Heledd's lament for Pengwern has turned into
jubilation, for the poet has seen the almond-tree with a
crown of snowy sheen on its head. He has also seen the Lamb
that was slain jumping in frolic over the world's horizon to a
new life; the sobbing of Paolo and Francesca has turned into
cheerful striving for the divine Order; the panoply of spring
and summer has arrived with daffodils and roses, the harvest
sun and the murmur of bees—they are all sensed in the vision
of the almond tree. There are two further stanzas, the last of
which voices a more personal conviction of gratitude. Précis
and paraphrase can give only a vague idea of the radiance of
diction achieved in this fine poem; they can give, perhaps,
an idea of the rich and varied imagery.

While *vers libre* is the favourite medium in the later
volumes, Pennar Davies has tried his hand on almost every
form, including the *englyn* and *cywydd,* the most popular
media in *cynghanedd.* The earlier volumes show a livelier
flair for experimentation. In recent years, although his lyric-
ism continues unabated, he has shown some dissatisfaction
with the shorter lyric forms and opted for lengthier and
more elaborate treatment. In *Yr Efrydd o Lyn Cynon* he
makes effective use of the ballad, characteristically loading it
with allegory and symbolism, partly in imitation of a

structure found in Dante's *Paradiso*. Some of the poems in *Cerddi Cadwgan* flirt with syncopated quarter-lines, and both here and elsewhere some of the longer forms are due to radio broadcasts, including a dramatic verse programme. There are some admirable sonnets, but the early triolets are among the poet's best technical achievements. One of these is doubly impressive in that it also gives vent, albeit with an attractive lightness of touch, to a theological dilemma which has long concerned his thinking on love:

> *Yn gyntaf oll pwy biau'r ias*
> *Ond Duw a'n gwnaeth mor frwnt, mor hyblyg?*
> *Er mwyn yr ias collasom ras:*
> *Yn gyntaf oll pwy biau'r ias?*
> *Pwy ond a wnaeth ein cnawd yn fras?*
> *Pwy ond a wnaeth ein rhyw yn ddyblyg?*
> *Yn gyntaf oll pwy biau'r ias*
> *Ond Duw a'n gwnaeth mor frwnt, mor hyblyg?*

(Whose, first of all, is the lustful urge, but God's, who made us so unclean, so unyielding? For the sake of the urge we have lost grace; whose, first of all, is the lustful urge? Whose but His, who made our flesh coarse, whose but His, who made our sex dual? Whose, first of all, is the lustful urge, but God's, who made us so unclean, so yielding?)

Here is a theme which is treated, in one way or another, in all six of the collections. I have referred above to some of the love poems and to the juxtaposition, in one couplet, of the Holy Spirit and the 'unashamed flesh'. There is a consistent approach based on the belief that if man is God-created, then his every instinct derives from Him. Implied also is a rejection of the traditional doctrine of man's Fall. 'Serch' ('Love'), a longish piece in the most recent volume, elaborates a series of reflections, beginning with the idea that there are two kinds of love, symbolized at first in the figure of

Esyllt or Isolde, who can command either the insensate
passion of the enslaved lover or, without her magic potion,
the pure adoration of one who stoops beneath her white
hands. The two kinds should be one, it is urged; their separation is a disease. Yet the poet goes on to rejoice that he has
achieved this unity; he has loved as Culhwch loved Olwen,
embracing with her the whole creation. The poem proceeds
on Arthurian and cosmic lines. Gwyn ap Nudd is on the side
of the seeker of integration:

> *Ynddo y mae'r llifogydd bywhaol,*
> *y greddfau gwyllt a thyner,*
> *y nwydau arswydus a glân.*

(In him are the life-giving streams, the wild and tender
instincts, the terrible and beautiful passions).

I do not care for the archaistic vocabulary in which some of
this poem is couched. Otherwise it is a welcome addition to
the many studies of love which give the poetry of Pennar
Davies, as indeed his novels and short stories, a unique
flavour in modern Welsh literature. Their confessional
honesty, their spiritual probing and their intellectual framework combine to make them highly distinctive. Many years
have passed since he published in *Y Llenor* a remarkable
piece of erotic analysis. It appears in *Naw Wfft* and is called
'Diffyg Traul' ('Indigestion'). It begins on a note of complaint:

> *Mae blwyddyn fach yn canlyn blwyddyn fach,*
> *a Duw a ŵyr beth sy'n ein hatal ni.*
> *A raid imi fyw am byth mor farwol grach,*
> *yn cydwastraffu'r neithdar gyda thi?*

(A little year follows a little year, and God knows what is
hindering us. Must I live for ever so mortally pettily,
wasting the nectar with you?)

There must be a better world than this, opines the narrator, - *nefoedd cydgnawdoliaeth lon,* 'the heaven of happy inter-fleshiness'. At this point it becomes clear that the nectar is male seed. The predicament is then clarified:

> *Dim problem ond y broblem fanwl, ddofn,*
> *problem gohirio hyd yr eithaf awr*
> *y cyffro rhythmig olaf; a dim ofn*
> *ond ofn yr ecstasi ardderchog fawr.*

(No problem but the precise, profound problem, the problem of postponing till the final hour the last rhythmic movement; and no fear but the fear of the splendid, great ecstasy).

In fact another problem is then mentioned, that of evoking a reciprocal orgasm. The animals must be laughing at us, it is said; *they* have long since mastered the art of love.

That the poet is conscious of criticism in this connection is clear from the poem to which he has given the Greek title 'Aletheia' ('Truth'). His answer is unequivocally Christian:

> *Nid hoff gan rai yw clywed*
> *Am nerth a rhinwedd rhyw.*
> *Ond Aletheia 'ddywed*
> *Mai'r Crëwr ydyw Duw.*
>
> *Os siociwyd rhai pan ddaethpwyd*
> *Ag oglau'r corff i'm llith,*
> *Gŵyr hi mai'r Gair a wnaethpwyd*
> *Yn gnawd ac nid yn rhith.*

(Some do not like hearing of the strength and virtue of sex, but Aletheia says that God is the Creator. If some were shocked when the odours of the body were brought into my writing, she knows that the Word was made flesh and not a wraith).

In his superbly rebellious and morally astringent *Naw Wfft* he attacks the bourgeois moderates for 'stuffing the mouth of the Crucified One and for castrating Pan':

Am stwffio genau'r Croeshoeliedig ac am ddisbaddu Pan.

While it is a far cry from the early agnosticism to the generous but militant Christian faith which has informed the poet's thinking, the intellectual element is present throughout. Sometimes it expresses itself in cool cerebration and semi-prosaic dialogue (as in 'Behemoth a Lefiathan'); and *Y Tlws yn y Lotws,* in spite of its embarrassment of imagistic riches, shows little of the sheer athletic vigour and pure inspiration of *Naw Wfft.* Attitudes remain firm. The poet's pacifism is as uncompromising as his nationalism; his internationalism is fervently cultural as well as political. His Christianity, as I have shown, is that of Christ rather than Paul; it is never exclusive and isolationist. Indeed *Naw Wfft* contains two quite captivating hymns to pagan gods—to the Aztec serpent-bird Quetzalcoatl and to the Nordic Balder. These hymns derive from 1940, and it was only then that Pennar Davies was experiencing his conversion to Christianity. Doubtless there are Christian suggestions in the prayer to the Aztec god:

> *Gwared ni rhag aur a gemau a gwisgoedd moethus.*
> *Gwared ni rhag celfyddyd er mwyn celfyddyd*
> *A thrythyllwch er mwyn trythyllwch.*
> *Gwared ni rhag Arglwyddi'r Angau.*

(Deliver us from gold and gems and sumptuous clothes. Deliver us from art for art's sake And lust for lust's sake. Deliver us from the Lords of Death).

Pennar Davies has applied the same imaginative sympathy

to our own pagan past. In his *Rhwng Chwedl a Chredo* he admirably expounds the ethos and idealism of our early myths and romances, showing how sadly this spiritual essence has been previously neglected. His poetic re-creation of some of these themes is a notable venture, and one is not surprised to find that there emerges an appealing relevance to the struggles of today.

THE POETRY OF ALUN LEWIS

David Shayer

What must strike anyone today who approaches the
literary achievement of Alun Lewis in anything more than a
cursory way is the stark contrast between the extent to which
informed and reputable opinion at the time of publication
accorded him praise of the highest kind, and the extent to
which his considerable qualities have been neglected subsequently. What critical assessment there has been has
centred almost exclusively on the 'war poet' aspect of Lewis,
and it is a fact that the wider consideration due to his poetry
has still not been made—indeed I feel, writing twenty-six
years after the publication of *Ha! Ha! Among the Trumpets*,
that proper critical attention to certain important (in my
opinion, central) aspects of his poetry is yet to be given. Of
course Lewis is to be seen as a Second World War poet, but
he is by no means just that, and there are themes and ideas
visible in the earliest poems which are to develop most intell-
igently and subtly in the later ones (culminating in 'The
Jungle' as one example) which, despite their original departure points, are not really immediately concerned with the
war situation at all. War or no war, one feels that Lewis
would eventually have travelled much the same road of
imaginative speculation to arrive at similar conclusions—

though we can never know the extent to which his search for a personal philosophy would have advanced in speculative and poetic terms had he been spared.

The word 'intelligent' is used advisedly; so many of the poems, stories and letters are distinguished by a striking intelligence, not merely in the academic sense (and Lewis took a first at Aberystwyth and was clearly extremely well read, poetically and otherwise) but an intelligence of feeling as well as of thinking, of intuitive response as well as of rational analysis. Lewis consistently reveals not only a keen awareness of surroundings and other people, but also a capacity for getting to the heart of things—of asking the right questions, as it were—with an eye for the significant which is as intelligent as it is imaginative.

I do not wish to indulge in idle speculation of a Romantic kind (what might he have written, how developed?) but there is in *Raider's Dawn* a range of subject matter, style, and metrical technique which suggests that his apprenticeship grounding was sufficiently wide to have permitted later development in a number of ways. We must be struck, for example, by the confident and rapid advance from the grimness of the industrial Welsh landscape to the colourful sensuality of the Mediterranean settings:

> *Our stubborn bankrupt village sprawled*
> *In jaded dusk beneath its nameless hills;*
> *The drab streets strung across the cwm,*
> *Derelict workings, tips of slag*
> *The gospellers and gamblers use*
> *And children scrutting for the coal*
> *The winter dole cannot purvey;*
> *Allotments where the collier digs*
> *While engines hack the coal within his brain . . .*

('The Mountain over Aberdare')

His artisans made me a palace of marble,
The ceilings they builded of beaten gold,
The walls they made lovely with lapis and amethyst
Chalcedony sardonyx amber and jade.

('The Captivity')

. . . Greasy Rhondda
River throws about the boulders
Veils of scum to mark the ancient
Degraded union of stone and water.

('The Rhondda')

. . . breathless wave
Kissing the sighing pebble-green,
Deep rock pools' trembling lucency
Through which the sunburnt Tyrian dives . . .

('War Wedding')

The Keats-like undertones in some of the earlier verse have already been noted (by John Stuart Williams, for example, in *The Anglo-Welsh Review* in 1964) and there is certainly a sense of self-indulgent sensuousness, even of mild decadence, in a poem such as 'The Captivity', though we know that Lewis is merely trying out a particular kind of Biblical style and is producing a piece of no great consequence. Occasionally—very occasionally—this sensual self-indulgence becomes vulgar in the way that the Keats of the 'slippery blisses' became vulgar: 'Stars seem gilded nipples/ Of the Night's vast throbbing breasts', but these lapses are fortunately rare. The potentially Romantic aspect of Lewis's Mediterranean interests are equally capable of expression in tough, even sardonic tones (see 'The Odyssey') and his treatment of love is never sublimated into cosily embarrassing cooings as some of the very early Keats was, but is always either convincingly and movingly tender or blatantly and splendidly erotic (as in 'War Wedding', 'The Madman', 'Fever', 'The Desperate' or 'Two Legends; for Greece')—though one would rather be without one or two of the more self-conscious terms, 'fain' for one.

Lewis's concern for carefully shaped metrical patterns, assonance, internal rhyme and so on can also be seen as a nineteenth century feature, but his skill in adapting these techniques to modern ends keeps the devices fresh as an integral part of his poetry without being self-consciously 'poetic'. His skill at pastiche is another matter; *Raider's Dawn* contains a number of interesting exercises in a variety of styles and much of what is obtrusively 'poetic' in the volume arises from the style of the imitated model:

> *Slim sunburnt girls adorn*
> *Lawns browsed by fawn and doe*
> *Through three long centuries this house*
> *Has mellowed in and known*
> *Only the seasonal fulfilment*
> *And the commemorated generations.*

('Lines on a Tudor Mansion)

Lewis is good at this sort of thing; lack of space prevents further consideration along these lines, but a study of his poems in terms of such techniques will reveal a most impressive craftsmanship.

Since the 'war poet' aspect is the best known let us begin with that;

> *All day it has rained, and we on the edge of the moors*
> *Have sprawled in our bell–tents, moody and dull as boors,*
> *Groundsheets and blankets spread on the muddy ground*
> *And from the first grey wakening we have found*
> *No refuge from the skirmishing fine rain . . .*

('All Day it Has Rained')

And next, the rough immediate life of camp
And barracks where the phallic bugle rules
The regimented orchestra of love;
The subterfuges of democracy, the stench
Of breath in crowded tents, the grousing queues . . .

('After Dunkirk')

Lewis did not, like Wilfred Owen, Edward Thomas, Graves and Sassoon, see war at its horrifying worst (though he came to the edge of a Japanese revelation which might have rendered their nightmares a pale shadow) and his poetry describes the 'phoney' war of camp training and troopship boredom with an emphasis on the gradual, cumulative attrition of individuality in the brutalising routine of army life, rather than on a once-for-all searing confrontation with active slaughter. It is perhaps for this reason that what war horror there is in *Raider's Dawn* — 'Odi et Amo', 'To a Comrade', 'Finale' — has strong '14-'18 overtones, even down to the mention of 'trenches'. However, the agonising experiences of parting from loved ones, of fear, of the anticipation of death itself are nonetheless vividly present in his writings, and we will not understand Lewis as a poet until we understand this Love-War, Life-Death axis at the heart of his poetry. Gweno and the war came together; the realisation of almost intolerable joy was almost exactly paralleled by a confrontation with the real possibility of death. There is a poem by Graves ('Pure Death') which expresses the dilemma exactly;

We looked, we loved, and therewith instantly
Death became terrible to you and me . . .

The lovers in Graves's poem, discovering for the first time what life can give, learn simultaneously the appalling loss which death would mean—and thus 'give' each other death. The war for Lewis becomes the death-dealing 'Beast', Gweno 'Beauty' (*In the Green Tree*, letter 17) each, with tragic irony, intensifying the other. The knife twist to this irony lies in the fact that as long as Lewis as lover and poet retains a keen and sensitive awareness of the one, he must retain an awareness of the other, and that to seek release from the pain which this situation entails in forgetfulness, numbness or indifference is to lose a little of the beloved's memory as well. (One suspects that there were times when the pain of this dilemma became so acute that Lewis saw death as a welcome release—a release from itself, in fact—though apart from directing attention to 'Burma Casualty' and to certain lines in the stories *Ward 03(b)* and *Dusty Hermitage*, I do not want to pursue this line of thought too far; Lewis was certainly interested in death in more than one way and by no means always in a despairing or fearful way.) This neutral ground of indifference lies between the intensities of Love and Death, and although it represents a zone of partial release it is a region where men cease to be full men, and where the poet—if he is not careful—can lose the keen edge of experience which is the only source, agonising or not, of his art. The creatures of nature, of course, the finches of 'The Soldier', the swifts of 'Lines on a Tudor Mansion', the kingfisher in 'The Jungle' are not afflicted thus and can teach man to lose himself in a surrender to instinctive immediacy, but then neither can they love nor feel as men do, not being blessed/cursed with human consciousness and all that it entails. The only long-term defence most of the men have against the reductive, insulting way of army life is to relapse into a coma of vegetable indifference;

> *Yet thought softly, morosely of them, and as indifferently*
> *As of ourselves or those whom we*
> *For years have loved, and will again*
> *To-morrow maybe love . . .*

('All Day it Has Rained')

And, as the crystal slowly forms,
A growing self-detachment making man
Less home-sick, fearful, proud,
But less a man . . .   ('After Dunkirk')

Lewis frequently uses the word 'dream' to describe this half-real world of retreat: 'wave and mist and dream', ('All Day it Has Rained'); 'Through daze and dream', ('The Soldier'); 'the dream/Emerging from the fact that folds a dream', ('To Edward Thomas'); 'But we who dream beside this jungle pool', ('The Jungle'). And, of course, it is the beloved who can wake the 'dreaming' poet—'For you abide,/A singing rib within my dreaming side', ('Post-Script:For Gweno')—as it is she who breathes life into his 'dying' or frozen body in 'War Wedding', 'Compassion' and 'Midwinter', or as Beauty redeems the wretchedness of 'the Beast'.[1]

The 'crystal' image in 'After Dunkirk' also occurs often enough in the poems to merit closer attention. Lewis seems to be saying that the mind cannot help but harden itself against army life, against the pain of separation, against the prospect of death—indeed it must so harden itself to remain sane—but it must remain clear enough for the man (or the poet) to keep the things that matter (love, 'real' life) in clear view. The danger is that the crystal may harden into excessive indifference and insensitivity and become a mirror of selfishness merely or self-pitying myopia which can remain as callous selfishness, or develop either into hysteria of a claustrophobic kind or into a casualness of a throw-away suicidal nature. At the beginning of 'The Soldier' the poet endures a nightmare of near-hysterical frustration, seeing the sunlight break 'its flashing wings/Imprisoned in the Hall of Mirrors'; in 'The Madman' the hysteria has achieved its climax with the ultimate loss of reason:

The shattered crystal of his mind
Flashes its dangerous splinters in the sun.

> *His eyes conceal behind their jagged smile*
> *The madness of his helplessness . . .*

'After Dunkirk' also refers to the despair

> *that nurtures self-contempt*
> *And makes men toss their careless lives away,*
> *While joy becomes an idiot's grin*
> *Fixed in a shaving mirror . . .*

Elsewhere, in 'Goodbye', a carafe of water becomes a crystal 'disclosing' the future, that is, it is seen *through*, and in 'A Troopship in the Tropics' there are those who still find among the unhappy, teeming decks some privacy in 'tranquil pools of crystal-clear reflexion'— not 'reflexion' as in a mirror, but as a memory penetrating back to the past.

The visual aspects of the involvement-indifference continuum are expressed in other ways; the poet must achieve just so much distance from the Love-Death intensities to enable him to contemplate them with clarity and deal with them artistically. This clarity is akin to clear but controlled sight. In 'To Edward Thomas' the poet wins a brief respite from the camp and climbs 'Thomas'' hill; here he can reflect with a vision which is keen but objective;

> *I sat and watched the dusky berried ridge*
> *Of yew trees, deepened by oblique dark shafts*
> *Throw back the flame of red and gold and russet . . .*
> *And sunlight with discerning fingers*
> *Softly explore the distant wooded acres,*
> *Touching the farmsteads one by one with lightness*
> *Until it reached the Downs . . .*
> *Where sight surrenders and the mind alone*
> *Can find the sheeps' tracks and the grazing.*

(It is true that at last sight must 'surrender' to the mysterious grey oblivion which holds death as its secret, but

human sight can never penetrate that mystery anyway.)
Where death is too insistent, too urgent, vision becomes distorted and blurred; in 'From a Play' the soldiers, after a day's
battle in a strange land

> *With the moon swaying across the river*
> *And black-headed kittiwakes and oyster-catchers*
> *Fishing the silver* . . .

remember their homes with moving clarity — until, in a
vision which blends moon and White Goddess and her
implacable sentence 'and no returning', the fact of Death impresses itself inescapably on them, and their 'sight' there-
after is blurred:

> *And now, on moonlit nights, we keep on seeing*
> *Our faint familiar homeland haloed*
> *In a rainbow of disease* . . .

The lovers in 'Raider's Dawn' cannot see beyond the drifting
snow of death (that death-snow neatly captured as 'lime'), in
'Parable' the soul must break 'the *blurred* delirious veils/Of
silence and of pathos and of self', in 'All Day it Has Rained'
the men are closed in upon themselves in a small circle of
rain 'wave and mist and dream', and in 'On Embarkation'
the departing men's eyes 'grow neutral in the long Unseen'.

The clear sight of objective contemplation is the necessary
basis for poetry, and to this extent all of Lewis's successful
poems are, whatever the intensity of their content, a triumph
of artistic stasis. Furthermore Lewis is not only aware of the
dream-coma or frantic hysteria which the soldier's trapped
situation can lead to, but at times deliberately reflects these
in the tone of his writing. The opening of 'The Soldier' has
been described as being exaggerated and uncontrolled:

> *I within me holding*

136

Turbulence and Time
— Volcanic fires deep beneath the glacier —
Feel the dark cancer in my vitals
Of impotent impatience grope its way
Through daze and dream to throat and fingers
To find its climax of disaster.

It seems clear that Lewis is deliberately using a wild, exaggerated style to reflect the state of the soldier's mind; the neat economy of the *second* section of the poem with its concrete simplicity similarly reflects the balance which that mind achieves in the contemplation of the finches' beauty (there is a similar deliberately melodramatic opening to 'The Madman' and an equally frantic intensity in 'Fever').

Here, in fact, is the poet's dilemma — how release the pain, the intensities of his experience, as controlled art and not as mad, jabbering incoherence? how is he to face the agony and retain its essence yet wrestle it into artistic shape? 'The Soldier' shows both the problem and its solution, and 'After Dunkirk' also explores the nature of the poetic problem in the situation of camp life;

I have been silent a lifetime
As a stabbed man,
And stolid, showing nothing
As a refugee.
But inwardly I have wept.
The blood has flown inwardly into the spirit . . .
But now I have this boon, to speak again . . .

Here the movement is inwards, the suffering turned *silently* in upon itself, but now the outward thrust of creative articulation (the poem) again becomes possible. 'After Dunkirk' describes the crystal beginning to form—the first stages of that crystallisation permitting poetic creativity or the outward gesture of the poem itself (which, with its carefully ordered sequence of ideas — 'First, then . . .', 'And

137

next . . . ', 'And then . . . ' — is a testimony to order and control). That these transitions between despair and hope represented the flux of Lewis's own experience is made clear in a letter quoted by Graves in his Foreword to *Ha! Ha! Among the Trumpets:* 'I live a certain rhythm which I'm becoming able to recognize. Periods of spiritual death, periods of neutrality, periods of sickening normality and insane indifference to the real implications of the present, and then for a brief wonderful space, may be every six weeks, a nervous and powerful ability moves upwards in me.'

There is in Lewis's poetry a strong association between (imaginative) creative expression and this idea of release, escape or bursting outwards. This struggle for release is explicitly sexual in 'Fever' ('Convulsed . . . I clamoured for relief'), in 'After Dunkirk' the imagination becomes the force that 'would pierce/Infinite night', and in 'Midwinter' the reaching out and bursting is embodied in the image of the breaking wave;

> *And when I came to the shore I felt you pull*
> *My heart as the passionate wave*
> *Answered the moontug, leaped, and in high poise*
> *Tense in a timeless curve contained itself,*
> *Then broke, ah broke, and shattered and seethed all white*
> *Upon the green and pebble beach* . . .

A wave, like a poem, is for a moment in time a shaped, fashioned curve of vital energy reaching outwards, but its power can only be so contained for a brief instant. There is also the implication of sexual ecstasy, a momentary experience of vision, unsustained; Lewis after all would have said that for him love and poetry were but different aspects of the same thing. The wave image appears again in 'A Separation',

The dead moon calls the sea
But the waves fall and break;
Their fall and break is a gesture
Of faith and of failure.

the sense of which is not so different from something Lewis
wrote in a letter to his wife (*In the Green Tree*, letter 4);
'. . . I can't reach it. Do you see how a poem is made — or
fails? By perpetually trying, by closer and closer failing, by
seeking and not finding, and still seeking, by a robustness in
the core of sadness'.

Graves has been mentioned several times and although
there is no evidence to suggest that Lewis was influenced to
any great extent by him there are a number of interesting
similarities between certain poems which are worth pointing to. There is, for example, the similar association of war
with wild beasts which demand blood sacrifices; in Lewis's
'Parable' the sabre-toothed hunter, coveting Soul's country,
gallops down 'Drunk with the blood of she-goats from the
hills. His drumming hooves excited primal terror . . . '; in
Graves's 'Outlaws' the 'old gods' lurk in the woods 'Starving
for unpaid dues: Incense and fire, salt, blood and wine / And
a drumming muse . . . ' There is the momentary verbal
echo from Graves's 'Haunted House' ('lust frightful') in
Lewis's 'Lines on a Tudor Mansion' ('Violence terrible');
both write 'Leda' poems and Odysseus poems; in 'Angry
Samson' Graves celebrated Samson alive and powerful
where in 'Lines on a Tudor Mansion' Lewis writes of
Samson dead; Lewis's 'Odi et Amo' contains a verse

Yet in this blood-soaked forest of disease
Where wolfish men lie scorched and black
And corpses sag against the trees . . .

which is similar (remembering that Lewis was experiencing
vicariously, not yet having seen active service) to the scene

described in Graves's 'Dead Boche'; Lewis's Moon Goddess in 'From a Play' is rather Graves-like, though Graves was not really to get his teeth into the goddess until after Lewis's death, and the hostile moon which wills the lovers apart at the beginning of 'War Wedding' has affinities with Graves's hostile moon in 'Full Moon'. Finally Lewis's favourite images of frost, darkness, star/glow-worm light — see 'Threnody' for example — may owe something to Graves's 'The Finding of Love'.

The other likely source behind a number of the *Raider's Dawn* poems is, of course, Edward Thomas, and there can be no question that one of the most important poems in the volume, 'The Sentry', owes much to Thomas's 'Lights Out'.

> *I have begun to die.*
> *For now at last I know*
> *That there is no escape*
> *From night . . .*
> *. . . I have left*
> *The beautiful lanes of sleep*
> *That barefoot lovers follow to this last*
> *Cold shore of thought I guard.*

(Lewis)

> *I have come to the borders of sleep*
> *The unfathomable deep*
> *Forest where all must lose*
> *Their way . . .*
> *Here love ends,*
> *Despair, ambition ends;*
> *All pleasure and all trouble . . .*

(Thomas)

Later Lewis wrote of his sinking into the 'death' darkness of the anaesthetic in Poona hospital: 'I have surrendered to what Edward Thomas foresaw—the land that he must leave and enter alone'.[2] Thomas's 'edge of the world' is a forest, black and silent, which must be entered alone; Lewis's is a 'cold shore', also black and silent.[3] In each poem the soldier, his 'former' life now a dream, faces the ultimate 'reality' of the darkness, and faces it with resolution. 'The Sentry' and 'From a Play' are linked by a passage in Lewis's journal: 'But slowly . . . we are achieving wisdom. Some in the violence and the subsequent desolation of night-bombed towns, *others in the quietness of the starry watch*, and in the day, unexpectedly after the thunder, they have seen Death—and it has made a difference to them.' (My italic.) The end of the short story *They Came* also shows a soldier doing solitary sentry duty at night on an 'upland ridge' (compare the 'sinister uplands' of 'From a Play') where he faces and accepts the challenge of total commitment to 'the world' and to Death at the expense of the personal.

This night or impenetrable blackness becomes a most potent symbol in Lewis's poetry for the mystery beyond human life, the ineluctable fact of death, beyond which there may or may not be something further. 'Threnody' suggests, though not all that convincingly, that life, light and regenerating warmth lie beyond death, and that as God first created life out of the cosmic darkness He will again breathe life into the frozen, dead soldiers who lie out under the seemingly indifferent night (a somewhat more hopeful version of Wilfred Owen's 'Futility' and similar in imagery). In *Ward 03(b)* Lewis describes soldiers 'losing ground along the whole front to the darkness that there is'; in 'Burma Casualty' the wounded officer sinks into the oblivion of the anaesthetic as into darkness, and later, returned to consciousness, remembers the comrades who have died in earnest, 'Thinking of all the lads the dark enfolds/So secretly'. In letter 28 Lewis also refers to sleep as 'darkness waiting to fold me away', and this sleep-death link is anticipated in 'The Sentry'—'the folded poppy/Night'—which must owe something to the Hamlet association between death and sleep. Of the final confrontation with death Lewis used the word 'consummation', and writing of a man lying critically injured with him in hospital he said: 'He also will be indifferent as to the greatest of all questions—to be or not to be', though Lewis seems to mean that the dying man has not only given up the struggle to live but is past puzzling over the mysteries of the 'undiscovered country' from which no one returns. In 'Threnody' Lewis describes

> *The white brain crossing*
> *The frontiers of darkness*
> *To darkness and always*
> *Darkness pursuing . . .*

which recalls Graves's 'Walk between dark and dark—a shining space' and Thomas's 'Out in the Dark':

> *How weak and little is the light,*
> *All the universe of sight,*
> *Love and delight,*
> *Before the might,*
> *If you love it not, of night.*

The ultimate darkness is also associated for Lewis with silence; the darkness is itself silent and enigmatic, and the men who confront it fall silent themselves. Under the arch of night 'The woman from the Egyptian rock-tomb . . . / Has taken the frozen soldiers into her silence'; 'And this glittering tree endure/This silence ever' ('Threnody'); 'Here, on this chasm . . . /I tremble in nightmares of silence' ('War Wedding'); 'Creation's silent matrix' ('Karanje Village'); 'And by that Arctic silence overawed/ The mind crawls wounded from the lidless God' ('In Hospital, Poona (2)'); 'The incantations of silence. God's

142

terrible silence' ('The Madman'). Where hope at last expires humanity waits 'In silence for the zero hour' ('After Dunkirk').

The opening of 'After Dunkirk' also describes Lewis himself as poet suffering in silence, and he almost certainly intended a contrast between the active, creative (fire-like) assertion of poetry writing and the cold dark silence of resignation, despair and death. As long as he can write poems and push these poems to the very edge of the darkness itself by facing it in the writing he is offering positive and defiant gestures of articulated (i.e. not silent) life-asserting art in the face of the ultimate silence. This seems to be the meaning behind the conclusion of the Introductory poem to *Raider's Dawn*, 'Prologue: The Grinder';

> *Keep grinding then, though nothing's left to whet —*
> *Bad luck unless your sparks can warm the night.*

Thus although Lewis is much concerned in his poetry, and is concerned at times in a despairing and apprehensive way, with both the ultimate 'cold shore' and with the darkness (which continues as a recurrent image in the Indian poems) the poems themselves constitute an answer to that final 'reality' which is a courageous embodiment of all that is vital, brilliant and warm (love's heat, as we have seen, being the inspiration of that creative process and standing as the antithesis of death). We would do well, in fact, in considering Lewis's poetry to remember that the specific content of the poems is only part of the picture, and that the creation of the poems themselves in the circumstances in which they were created is a fact of equal importance. Those who have tended to emphasise the 'darkness' side of the poetry (John Davies, for example, in *The Anglo-Welsh Review*, 1970) have perhaps not always realised just how subtle a poetic game Lewis is playing nor the extent to which he is acting as

an obstinate poetic spokesman for what is positive, enduring and vital in human experience — what matters is not the
fact that the darkness exists but what he *does* about it. It is
true that he needs help (love's strength) and that there is at
least one occasion where the darkness is described as closing
in to force a temporary silence ('War Wedding' section I) but
— certainly up to the time of his death — the darkness is kept
firmly, if uneasily, at bay. What is so appropriate about the
choice of 'Prologue: The Grinder' as the introductory poem
to *Raider's Dawn* is that it embodies its own message (it *is*
the spark that challenges the night) and thus represents in
miniature Lewis's principal poetic intention.

To see the poet as defiant bearer of fire in a dark and frozen
world is to see him in the role of Prometheus, and the
opening of 'War Wedding' suggests that Lewis was aware of
the association. (It is also interesting to recall that Shelley's
Prometheus was nailed to his rock amid the deadness of
black winter without 'shape or *sound* of life.'[4]) Death is
cold; the corpses are frozen in 'Threnody', the soldier faces a
cold shore in 'The Sentry', the lovers in 'Raider's Dawn' see
the dead as drifting snowflakes, and in 'Peace' Peace herself
lies inert in the grip of winter;

> *The wind blows*
> *Through her eyes,*
> *Snow is banked*
> *In her whiter thighs* . . .

Lewis wrote to his wife: 'I find myself quite unable to express at once the passion of Love, the coldness of Death
(Death is cold) and the fire that beats against resignation . . . ' 'Threnody' does suggest that beyond the frost
of death there can be a reawakening to a new life (that there
is a supranatural answer) and in 'Peace' the stirrings of new
plant life and of Spring are described as beginning in the

depths of midwinter (that there is a seasonal 'natural' answer). The theme of new fire and thaw also lies at the heart of 'Midwinter', and here it is the beloved who unfreezes the poet's heart which is likened to a frozen wave. The link between this image and the poetic process itself has been noted already; a frozen wave-heart is no good, nor, by analogy, is a shapeless raving torrent. The poet walks through the winter landscape;

I took the path to the sea along the ruts
Whose crystals cracked and crunched beneath my
boots . . .
The disused quarry, red with peat and iron,
Suspended frozen stalactites of moss.
The briars' vernal thrust
Writhed vainly in the ice womb of the soil . . .
And I like the grass cried out
In the ice of your absence . . .

The outward thrust of the briars is frustrated, and nature's cry is silenced—or rather nature gives a 'silent' cry, like the poet; the paradox is continued as the meadows scream 'dumbly' and earlier in the poem an old countryman remarks of the frozen waves 'It is indeed/Funny to hear that silence'. The beloved comes like a blessing, the blessing of rain and thaw which restores articulation ('the loosening laughter of rain'); she revives his 'flame' (allowing the poem to be written—like 'After Dunkirk' 'Midwinter' describes the process necessary for its own creation) and brings him to warmth and love while the frozen fields thaw 'And the river runs again with gladness to the sea'. Perhaps Edward Thomas's 'Like the touch of rain she was/On a man's flesh and hair and eyes' is somewhere there in the background, or even 'Western wind, when wilt thou blow,/The small rain down can rain?'. Thomas's 'It Rains' contains a number of images which Lewis also uses elsewhere — two lovers walking and kissing ('The Soldier'), rain and twilight ('All Day it Has Rained'), and in the dark the glowing white of the flower ('Threnody'). In 'Midwinter' it is the beloved who releases the frozen wave-heart of the poet and enables the outward sweep and flow, the reach of creative articulation to follow. She it is whose breath 'rekindles' life (compare 'Corfe Castle'—'Quicken the dying island with your breath' or 'Compassion'—'In the meadows of her breath') as it is she who raises the poet from death to life in 'War Wedding'.

Lewis considered 'War Wedding' to be the best poem in the *Raider's Dawn* collection and there is some justification for this view. It is one of the most richly allusive of the early poems and contains some of his best lyrical passages; the seven linked sections with their close-knit, at times almost cryptic style combine to form a unified and convincing whole and exhibit an impressive range of ideas. The poem, obviously occasioned by the bitter-sweet experience of Lewis's war-time marriage, makes use of certain (Greek) mythological references to give an additional dimension to the very personal nature of the subject.[5] The starting point is his wife's name, Gweno-Venus, explicit in Section IV 'He gives her Botticelli's Birth of Venus as a Wedding Gift'; in a letter to Jean Gilbert[6] we find 'Elle s'appelle Gweno (c'est Gallois, en francais Venus!—moi, je suis un petit satellite de Mars . . . '). Subsequently he identifies himself not only with Mars (he is now in the army) but also with another of Venus's celebrated lovers, Adonis.[7]

Section I shows the soldier-poet in the barrack room at night, waiting for the beloved and near death. Given the Venus background and the frequent linking in other poems of the war/army with 'the beast' it seems that he lies spiritually bleeding to death of a wound inflicted by the beast as Adonis was wounded ('shambles of my love', 'Into the gutters of darkness I bleed and bleed'). Already the darkness begins to claim him. The sun (to be interpreted as the male principle opposed by the withered female moon who denies the love, and also as the Promethean fire-creative principle— as the flame fades the poet falters into silence; 'And here the hiatus falls, the stammer . . . ') is eaten by the bird of death; the light first 'gutters' and is then wiped out completely in the eclipse that follows. Sinking from the light the poet comes to a 'chasm' of darkness and his last cry is the beloved's name. In Section II ('She tarries, far-off, in a strange anguish') the woman has a vision of her lover torn and ripped in sea terms ('Salted and pierced sucked-in side', 'ripped to sea-weed shreds') while there is also in her vision an unmistakable reference to Christ, broken and torn ('pierced . . . side', 'Oh. Had I only slid my nails/Into your gaping cicatrice') and she has clearly failed or denied him in some way ('And cockcrow rips the lie out of my brain'). The Christ references are continued later with the emphasis on rising from death ('I rise' Section III) and in the Communion reference in V ('We are the bread and wine who share the feast'). The sea images, of course, point beyond Christ and imply death by water as well as death by mutilation-wounding. Although Adonis did not die by water his festival was celebrated in the Mediterranean coast cities, particularly in the Phoenician city of Byblus which was renowned throughout the ancient world as the centre of the Venus-Adonis cult, by the throwing of his mangled effigy into the sea, out of which he 'rose' again. The Adonis cult of death-resurrection has several points in common with the Christ story and Sir James Frazer has suggested that the Adonis and Christ stories were different versions of the same myth, Adonis 'becoming' Christ as Christianity refashioned the old cults.[8] There is also identification between Christ and the ordinary soldier (and therefore with Lewis himself) in 'Finale', where the officer is 'Crucified on a cross of fire', and in 'Threnody' where 'Countless humble peasant Christs' are slaughtered.

There is a further, though more fanciful, line of thought here, which centres on the origin of Venus's birth. Cronos castrated his father Uranus and threw the severed member into the sea where the foam around it formed Venus's body (she also 'rises' from the sea). Cronos also sacrificed his son to save the country in time of war (the war against the Titans). According to Frazer Cronos was called 'Israel' by the Phoenicians, and he took his 'only begotten son' and sacrificed him upon an altar 'in time of war, when the country was in great danger from the enemy'. There is thus a direct link between Venus, Cronos, Cronos as Israel, Christ as Israel's son sacrificed for the general good, and the ordinary soldier (Lewis himself) called upon by his country to make, if necessary, the supreme sacrifice in a time of national danger.

In Section III the beloved at last comes to the poet, but not until he is in the sleep of death. Now *she* becomes 'the saviour' who will 'touch the blindness from my eyes' and restore him to light, life and manhood (as she rekindles life, also as Cytherea, in 'Midwinter'). She beckons the poet and he rises, leaving the sleeping army behind; 'And I rise from the restless armies/That cough like huddled sheep'—this, with the 'dreaming German soldier' who must first be encountered, is almost certainly an echo of Wilfred Owen's 'Strange Meeting' ('It seemed that out of battle I escaped') where he meets his 'dreamt German', and it reinforces the idea that the poet, like Owen's soldier, and like Adonis, is now in hell. The beloved raises the poet from the underworld, 'starts the shrivelled heart' and lifts him to the upper regions, beckoning in 'infinite space' (the physical consummation will follow in Section V). This ascent and escape is only temporary, however; at the end of the poem the poet has to leave his love and return to the 'underworld' of war; 'But now the reaper shaves his head/And goes to harvest with the dead/Far from the pastures of his fond desire.' (Section VII). Adonis, who was associated with seasonal renewal and fertility, was doomed to spend half the year in the lower regions of Hades. He would have remained there permanently if Venus herself had not followed him down, won him from the dark powers, and lifted him to life and love for half the year.[9] Adonis's annual 'resurrection' occurred in the spring and the lovers' consummation in V is associated with 'the green leash of her Spring/ And flowers blossom . . . '; there is the 'thrust/Of natural fertility' (followed, significantly, by 'And Gods who shivered in the dust/Have found their lost divinity'); and there is the child born of the love (Section VII) 'She said I made her fertile with a smile'.

Section IV with its sea imagery, shells and anemone (which were sacred to Venus) is devoted to the beloved, seen as Love's personification;

Whorled periwinkle, breathless wave
Kissing the sighing pebble-green,
Deep rock-pools' trembling lucency
Through which the sunburnt Tyrian dives
For the pearl in its dark yolk . . .

It is apt that here the 'rising' of the woman—Venus's emergence from the sea to take her place among the gods as depicted by Botticelli—should match the 'resurrection' of the man which she herself has accomplished, and that in the next Section the two should meet as 'risen equals' in a communion of ecstasy. This fifth Section, 'The Marriage Bed', is a moving love lyric, tender and sensual;

Draw a green cedar over the peeping sky,
Latch the grey sash across the glancing sea,
Close the dark door and lie within the rose,
Beloved, lie with me.

Both are now resurrected, both united in mutual communion and mutual salvation, which is an achievement of godhead in both a Greek mythological and Christian sense; 'We are the bread and wine who share the feast;/The elements are in our nakedness'. In Section VI their last hours together slip away, and with daybreak in Section VII the poet must return to the war. The beloved is left to muse upon the ugly futility of it all;

> *The city changes hands by day and night*
> *A whore for whom the drunkards fight.*
>
> *Where Love surrenders in that brawl*
> *Their names are scrawled in blood along the wall.*

The Love-Death poles are at the heart of the poem; war with its foul images ('the soiled red tourniquet', 'shambles', 'scream', 'eagles of suffering') stands in stark contrast to the bright sea, flowers, flowing hair and beauty associated with and surrounding Love herself who raises the suffering soldier out of the horror to light and life, though his respite is only a short one. The range of imagery and tone is most impressive and Lewis has produced a fine piece of evocative writing. We have, in effect, the method of 'Threnody' but here enriched by the mythic patterns which lend a greater degree of depth to the poem and give a sense of utilised 'tradition' in the Eliot sense — personal and universal, modern and mythic being blended into a single imaginative statement.

Of all the quotations included so far one of the most important from the point of view of tracing Lewis's speculative development is that from 'The Madman'—'The incantations of silence, God's terrible silence'. Lewis's probing of this mental and spiritual enigma at the edge of life, and his formulation of possible answers to the mystery at the heart of existence is an important thread running through his writing. We have already noted the ostensibly optimistic conclusion of 'Threnody', but this poem is exceptional in *Raider's Dawn* with its introduction of a beneficent Deity who answers the cold-dark death negation which dominates the poem. Elsewhere Lewis wrote (of a discussion with a friend in Poona Hospital): ' . . . we talked of Hindu rein-carnation ideas and Christian life after death and they as usual failed to mean anything to me . . . '[10] and else-where: 'The infinite, of which I can never be sure, is God the Maker . . . No attempt has been made to convince me— neither by man nor God' (see Graves's Foreword to *Ha! Ha!*). In the face of God's silence Lewis turns to the tangible particularities of the here and now, 'the ostrich's eggs warming in' the sun' as he put it, and he celebrates the beauties of the natural world with a passionate intensity;

> *My soul cries out with love*
> *Of all that walk and swim and fly.*
> *From the mountains, from the sky,*
> *Out of the depths of the sea*
> *Love cries and cries in me.*

> ('Odi et Amo')

Yet despite this he is aware (and 'The Madman' is a sensitive exploration of the theme) that the physical world is not by itself 'adequate'. 'The Madman' describes a world of physical beauty, ramifying outwards from the minuteness of the sea-shell to mountains and skyscapes;

> *Developing through the countless variations*
> *Of branches and skylines and streams winding,*
> *Through perfect mutations of mountain and cloud and*
> *cattle . . .*

151

But we cannot possess the essence of this universe, the essence we call 'life'—we touch the flower but cannot capture its bloom;

> *The sensual mind in the wreathes of wine*
> *Deflowers with its touch the tangible,*
> *But cannot save the bloom, the dust, the pollen,*
> *The glow of beauty, its soft immanence . . .*

Life is like 'a beautiful girl who loves no one'; we may strive to seize life, may strive for the all-comprehending vision (as in Blake's 'Crystal Cabinet'—'I strove to seize the inmost form/With ardour fierce and hands of flame . . . '—Lewis here links 'vision' with sexual ecstasy) and indeed think we have it, yet our seemingly stupendous and earth-shaking experience is merely 'a lover's gesture' (a physical gesture) and the vision exists only in man's mind, a mind which fully extended is no more than 'an inarticulated question' unable to begin to frame the right enquiries in the face of 'The incantations of silence, God's terrible silence'.

It could be argued that 'Threnody' is not in fact the only optimistic poem on this theme in *Raider's Dawn* and that both 'The Humanist' and 'The East' are equally confident. The joke behind 'The Humanist' is that God used Crivelli's genius anyway, despite the artist's more matter of fact view of the situation ('The Church paid well') but the poem is not serious enough to bear comparison with 'Threnody'. 'The East' is, however, and this poem must be read in conjunction with 'The Crucifixion' in *Ha! Ha!* 'The East' can be quoted in full:

> *If passion and grief and pain and hurt*
> *Are but the anchorite's hair-shirt,*
> *Can such a torment of refining*
> *Be aimless wholly, undesigning?*

Must
Such aching
Go to making
Dust?

Whispered the wind in the olive tree
In the garden of Gethsemane.

Now I cannot help but feel that this is ambiguous; of course it could be read as an assertion of Christ's eternal reality and triumph over suffering (which is given purpose by that triumph) but it could also be read—and the poem does not answer its own question—as a testimony to the poet's continuing uncertainty and lack of conviction. 'The Crucifixion' seems to strengthen the latter possibility. It is true that Christ's agony on the cross 'this awful hanging/ Obscene with urine, sagging on a limb' is described as being 'not the end of Life', but the intense preoccupation in the poem with that suffering ('Breaking his Self up', 'every throbbing stigma', 'The pangs that puffed and strained his stomach wall') together with the ominous placing of 'and improved nothing' as the concluding words of the poem, must suggest that Lewis is unconvinced, or at least only partially convinced, that there is a point to it all and that the agony does not simply go to the making of dust and absolutely nothing else. Undoubtedly the crucial question in the poem is Lewis's question in the face of his own possible death; one can go to meet the end confidently and courageously as Christ did, but, when the death torment envelops one, does the nerve crack, does confidence evaporate, does one, when it is too late, suddenly realise the appalling truth that death is not a beginning but the end of everything?

The impact which India had upon Lewis certainly did not make his search for understanding any easier. The title of his second anthology he took from Job, Chapter 39, adding (in letter 36) 'sarcastic-like'. Presumably he meant to compare himself with the horse described in that passage who laughs fearlessly and defiantly in the thick of the battle, but the main theme of this 39th Chapter is a celebration of the natural beauty of God's creatures— wild goat, unicorn, peacock, ostrich, horse, hawk and eagle—whose strength and instinctive splendour man cannot hope to understand or emulate; he can only wonder at these things and abase himself before their mysterious Creator. The passage is thus central to the particulars-infinite debate in 'The Madman'. We know that when he went to India Lewis had read E.M.Forster's *A Passage to India* since letter 27 describes him re-reading it, and there may be a reference to Forster's Marabar Caves incident in one of Lewis's first Indian poems, 'By the Gateway of India, Bombay'—

> *Where pilgrims walked on naked feet:*
> *— And in the darkness did they see*
> *The darker terrors of the brain?*
> *And did the hollow oracle resound*
> *In caves of unexpected pain?*

Forster's theme, of course, is precisely that appalling silence on God's part which Lewis has already explored on his own account. Man is trapped in the spherical cave of an indifferent universe and deludes himself that his projections and the echoes and reflections of those gestures and utterances exist in their own right, when in fact the cosmic indifference around him makes no distinction between the logical or the illogical, the pleasurable or the painful, the good or the evil. The misery, famine and wretchedness which Lewis saw in India he saw against the backcloth of a silent and utterly unresponsive universe;

But the people are hard and hungry and have no love
Diverse and alien, uncertain in their hate,
Hard stones flung out of Creation's silent matrix . . .

('Karanje Village')

As in Godbole's song[11]the gods do not return to earth, they do not come to relieve men's suffering or to renew the burntout land;

Who is it climbs the summit of the road?
Only the beggar bumming his dark load.
Who was it cried to see the falling star?
Only the landless soldier lost in war.

And did a thousand years go by in vain?
And does another thousand start again?

('The Mahratta Ghats')

(It is not just 'The East' that asks questions.) India seemingly offered Lewis 'reality' with all the comforting compromises stripped off. He wrote to Gravés: 'It is easy to write prose in India . . . But poetry is harder to command, mainly I think because everything is somehow remorseless here, arid, pellucid and incurable' and elsewhere he refers to 'the sterile fires of this land' ('The River Temple') and to 'the nihilist persistence of the sun' ('Assault Convoy').

Lewis's reaction to India, if so crude a term may be used, was however by no means one of despair—on the contrary the misery of India clearly led him into new regions of sympathy for his fellow men and deepened an already pronounced capacity for compassion. At the heart of this compassion lay strength, and at the heart of the strength lay love—his love for his absent wife — and love becomes the supremely simple answer for the human condition as he saw it. The simplicity of this truth lies behind 'To Rilke', but what distinguishes India is a tragic absence of love — climate, poverty and division denying 'The love that is imprisoned in each heart' ('Indian Day');

> *Love could be had for nothing.*
> *And where is love now?*
> *Gone with the shambling oxen,*
> *Gone with the broken plough,*
> *Death lives here now.*

('Observation Post')

The experience of the Vishnu statue described in 'To Rilke', 'Karanje Village', and in the Journal passage quoted by Hamilton[12] was clearly a significant event for Lewis, a moment of insight or brief vision of some kind related to a fuller realisation of the experience of living;

> *And alone by a heap of stones in the lonely salt plain*
> *A little Vishnu of stone,*
> *Silently and eternally simply Being*
> *Bidding me come along.*

('Karanje Village')

This simplicity of 'Being' is somehow tied up with the simplicity of love, and 'To Rilke' actually says as much:

> *And Vishnu, carved by some rude pious hand,*
> *Lies by a heap of stones, demanding nothing*
> *But the simplicity that she and I*
> *Discovered . . .*

(Was Rilke one of his wife's favourite poets? She taught

German and in letter 9 Lewis tells her he has been reading
'your' Rilke—which would strengthen the pattern of associations in the poem.)

Not surprisingly the love poems from India assert love's
constancy and persistence with unremitting conviction;
' . . . Time upon the heart can break/But love survives the
venom of the snake' ('In Hospital: Poona (I)'); 'But love and
beauty will survive/These grey malignant hours'
('Shadows'). Love is, of course, 'out' of time (compare
'Raider'sDawn'where the lovers are 'Slaves of Time' but also
'Eternity's masters'); the Fall brought mankind under time's
rule, but love between man and woman can overcome this
curse.[13] ·Shadows', the second and third verses of which have
echoes of 'War Wedding', asserts light and love against
darkness and time's remorseless passage;

> *The moon turns round the earth*
> *And the earth turns round the sun;*
> *In gold and white infinities*
> *Their timeless task is done.*

But although the earth may throw the moon periodically
into shadow, and although every turn of the earth brings
darkness to part of its surface, the sun is still there, a
triumphant constant. The very nature of existence itself, the
poem insists, is a light-dark-light cycle, and the placing of
'timeless' in the first verse and the fact that it is 'light' which
concludes the poem (not 'dark') underline the optimism of
its intention; darkness, like a parting, is an absence, a
negative merely, not a positive.

The imagery of 'Shadows' is also to be seen with fine effect
in 'In Hospital: Poona(I)';

> *Last night I did not fight for sleep*
> *But lay awake from midnight while the world*

Turned its slow features to the moving deep
Of darkness, till I knew that you were furled,
Beloved, in the same dark watch as I.

The 'turning' or wheel image occurs a number of times in
the Indian writings, and may owe something to the Hindu
wheel of reincarnation. The idea is implicit in the conclusion of 'The Mahratta Ghats' ('And did a thousand years
go by in vain?/And does another thousand start again?') and
in the lines from 'Village Funeral'—'How shall the peasant
fare between/One birth and another birth?'. Explicit wheel
images include 'the wheeling spokeshave of the stars',
'distance spun for ever in the mind' ('The Journey')
' . . . the stars/Wheeling beyond our destiny' ('The
Jungle'); in letter 22 we find: 'I don't know why this
particular batch of new faces and things should make me sad
and disconsolate . . . I suppose it's just a turn in the
wheel'; and in letter 34: 'I shall be sorry to leave (here) but the
wheel turns and we turn with it.'

Lewis's struggle to understand the nature of human existence is carried further in 'The Jungle' which is one of the
most satisfying poems in *Ha! Ha!* It is an interesting feature
of the poem that although it relates to new experiences
(Lewis's first encounter with the Burmese jungle geographically, new ideas imaginatively) it contains images
which have not been used since *Raider's Dawn,* including
the 'dream' image, and the idea of the natural world's instinctive but limited 'rightness' and Lewis has succeeded in
lifting the jungle scene and his own reaction to that scene to
a level of universal significance. The opening of the poem
suggests that we are in a Fallen world, a fallen (autumnal)
paradise garden, which decays and rots and exudes a sinister
languor.

In mole-blue indolence the sun
Plays idly on the stagnant pool
In whose grey bed black swollen leaf
Holds Autumn rotting like an unfrocked priest.

The section is steeped in the Earth-Water downward pull of decaying physical matter—and these two elements have always been associated with the Fall—which tempts man into an indolent, mindless, spiritless surrender of a vegetable kind, into 'The green indifference of this sleep'. The second section likens the world at large and its cities with their streets, parks, offices and citizens, to this trackless, confused 'lost' jungle area, where men have mislaid their way and where war compounds the tragic confusion.[14] In the third section *man* is considered—man who carries the confusion in his heart, whose capacity for good is inextricably tied (in his Fallen nature) to a capacity for evil, and whose happiness is always a hairsbreadth away from misery;

The vagueness of the child, the lover's deep
And inarticulate bewilderment,
The willingness to please that made a wound,
The kneeling darkness and the hungry prayer;
Cargoes of anguish in the holds of joy
The smooth deceitful stranger in the heart,
The tangled wrack of motives drifting down
An oceanic tide of Wrong.
And though the state has enemies we know
The greater enmity within ourselves.

Yet man is consistent in some things and retains a fragment at least of his pre-Fall simplicity; 'Some things we cleaned like knives in earth,/Kept from the dew and rust of Time/Instinctive truths and elemental love . . . ' The reference to the instinctive trust of the teal and quail who seem to obey

some greater force in their migration over the Himalayas—as
man seemingly obeys some greater force in these instinctive
loves and truths—may owe something to the Job Chapter:
'Doth the hawk fly by thy wisdom, and stretch her wings
towards the south?'

This constancy in inconstancy leads on to the pool metaphor, where man sees in the water the fallen image of
himself as a distortion of his unfallen, ideal face; 'The face
distorted in a jungle pool/That drowns its image in a mort
of leaves'—which carries a wealth of death-Fall meaning in
its 'drowns', 'mort' and 'leaves'. Section four continues this
line of thought, re-emphasising the 'ghostly' nature of man,
wandering bewildered in his lost paradise garden, yet again
answering this despair with the reminder of man's capacity
to glimpse from time to time a vision of the ideal, a vision of
the possible which seems momentarily to shake time's
oppressive grip on us:

And sudden as the flashing of a sword
The dream exalts the bowed and golden head
And time is swept with a great turbulence,
The old temptation to remould the world.

The irony of the word 'temptation' is almost painful; to be
'tempted' thus, as fallen beings, is in a sense our salvation,
raising us above ourselves—yet it was just such a temptation
to 'remould the world' which caused the Fall in the first
place.

Then comes the climax of the poem, and of Lewis's
personal quest for certainty; does the pre-Fall ideal, the
potential paradise, the state of constant truth, unmarred
love and man's best self exist somewhere beyond and above
us as a reality in its own right or does it exist merely in our
own minds? Does anything exist beyond death? Is the
Paradise story a myth which we have invented, a testimony

to our better selves, merely? (Significantly Lewis introduces at this point that characteristic image of cosmic silence and indifference — coldness; 'cold with space'). Does the individual soul achieve at death its lost state and do we struggle for the ideal as for a certain future goal?

> *Or does the will's long struggle end*
> *With the last kindness of a foe or friend?*

the good existing only in mankind's own nature, nowhere else, and dying with him? Is there, behind the death of any and every individual, a cosmic harmony and plan? 'Then would some unimportant death resound/With the imprisoned music of the soul?' The Platonic aspect of this is unmistakable; also in letter 19 Lewis wrote: 'It seems to me that wherever I go the world over I meet people somewhere or other who are lovely and animated conceptions of some original and beautiful idea. I like to feel that is so, anyway.'

As in 'The East' and 'The Mahratta Ghats', 'The Jungle' does not answer the questions it poses, indeed it concludes with three unanswered questions.One feels that Lewis is now seeking truth not only on his own, but also on mankind's behalf, yet despite the extension of compassion which this concern carries with it, the mystery is no nearer penetration.

When Graves warned Lewis against 'democratic' irrelevancies in his poetry, Lewis wrote to Richard Mills,[*] 'I wrote back and said that my whole power, such as it is, springs from one source — humility — which alone engenders and resolves my perpetual struggle against the arrogant and the submissive, the victors and the vanquished.' Now the possession of real humility will prevent not only arrogance and presumption but also self-pity and submission (which is the reverse face of pride). What was vital to Lewis was 'integrity and *willingness to endure*' and 'The Jungle' makes clear the

connection in his mind between submission, surrender and
dream-like inactivity and the worst aspects of man's fallen
nature. Poetry, as we have seen, was very much a gesture of
defiant 'endurance' for him, and his own humility is
revealed in his approach to the great questions concerning
the mysteries of human existence and the honesty with
which he faces them, in his gratitude for the beauties of
nature and the blessings of the physical world, in his gratitude for his wife's love and in his own capacity to endure the
trials of active service with patience (see 'Parable' for
example, or the several references to uncomplaining acceptance[16]). There is also the sympathy for the suffering Indian
peasants, the admiration for their capacity to endure and go
on living, and the conviction that these people wanted 'the
same things I do'. It seems clear that this capacity to endure
life's less pleasant offerings with patience, and extract from
the experience a heightened compassion rather than an increased selfishness, an extension of sympathy for others out
of one's own pain rather than an increased self-centredness,
lies at the heart of Lewis's artistic achievement—an achievement characterised by the blend of intelligence and
sympathy which I have attempted to make explicit in this
brief survey. I do not wish to pretend that Lewis was a major
poet (though he was certainly an important minor one) and
there can be no escaping the fact that, as with all poets at the
outset of their careers, we will find a number of the published poems to be unconvincing, artificial or unhappily
pretentious ('Corfe Castle' and 'Westminster Abbey' are
singularly unmemorable, and the long 'On Embarkation' is
a very uneven poem, dull in parts and doggedly prosaic).
The fact remains that Lewis offers us a handful of poems
that are first-rate, and moreover a consistency of theme and
interest which indicates that we are dealing with something
more than a merely occasional or week-end writer.
Romantic, in the best sense, as many of the poems are, with

their basis in a passionate, personal encounter with love and with the mutability implications of that encounter, the seriousness of, for example, 'The Madman', 'Crucifixion', 'Karanje Village', 'Burma Casualty' or 'The Jungle' points to a talent of much wider proportions. There is also in Lewis's poetry a serious concern for the nature of poetry itself, an awareness of what the act of poetic creation can mean in the face of a chaotic and destructive world, and an attempt to use the poem as thing-in-itself to convey the poet's fundamental message—something which in itself will not make poor poems great ones, but which must influence our approach to the poet on the side of respectful judgment.

To see Lewis merely as a minor and uncomplicated latter-day Romantic going through the poetic motions required by 'love' and 'war' as they act upon a youthful sensibility is to see only a fraction of the truth. Lewis's maturity, his intelligence and his awareness of the nature and importance of artistic exploration make him a much more interesting figure, indeed the subtlety of much of his material and the proficient and calculated way in which he handles it deserve considerable respect. The question may be idle, but is forgivable; what enquiries, metaphysical and artistic, might he have been pursuing today?

Notes.
1.   War is associated with Beasts in 'Parable', 'War Wedding', and 'The Way Back', and in 'Two Legends: for Greece' the Minotaur Beast's influence pales before the innocence of a girl.
2. Hamilton, I., *Alun Lewis*, 1966, p.52.
3. Rupert Brooke was rather fond of dark shores for a time, see 'The Song of the Beasts' and 'Seaside'.
4.   The lines from 'In Hospital: Poona (2)', 'And by that Arctic silence overawed/The mind crawls wounded from the lidless God' also clearly echoes images from the opening

section of *Prometheus Unbound*.

5. That Lewis was interested in mythology is clear from 'Parable', 'Two Legends; for Greece', 'The Odyssey', 'The Swan's Way', and 'Jason and Medea'.

6. Hamilton, I., op.cit., p.20.

7. Lewis has another Adonis poem - see 'Two Legends; for Greece'.

8. There is another 'sea resurrection' described elsewhere in Lewis's poetry:

> *I sank in drumming tides of grief*
> *And in the sea-king's sandy bed*
> *Submerged in gulfs of disbelief*
> *Lay with the redtoothed daughters of the dead.*
>
> *Until you woke me . . .*

('Midnight in India')

9. A descent on the beloved's part to the side of the man seems to be intended also in 'Midwinter', where, addressing her as Cytherea, the poet bids her speak 'Of your troubled voyaging down/Through the chasms of time and pain,/Of the stress of the rocks on your soul,/And your soul's escape'.

10. Hamilton, I., op.cit., p.52.

11. *Passage to India*, Chap.7.

12. Hamilton, I., op.cit., p.46.

13. 'the venom of the snake' carries us back to the Fall, and see also the song 'Oh Journeyman' with its lines 'Life has trembled in a kiss/From Genesis to Genesis'.

14. The theme, with its 'fallen' jungle setting as a microcosm of the world is the same as William Golding's in *Lord of the Flies*.

15. Hamilton, I., op.cit., p.34.

16. 'And stifled our antipathies' ('From a Play'); 'The difficult tolerance of all that is/Mere rigid brute routine', 'I have been silent a lifetime . . . / . . . stolid, showing nothing', '. . . one learns to bear/Insult as quietly as if it were /A physical deformity' ('After Dunkirk').

THE POETRY OF GWYN THOMAS

Elan Clos Stephens

Literary criticism in Wales recently has been much concerned with the aesthetic poetic versus a rationalistic poetic; 'the concept', as Dafydd Elis Thomas put it in the first Triskel volume of essays 'of the poem as a structure rather than as yet another form of direct linguistic communication.' This sort of debate is not simply a power-struggle between the University poet and *y bardd gwlad*, the *bardd tywyll* and the versifier. It begs the question of differences within the 'mainstream'/University based poetic itself. For instance, to adopt the principle of the aesthetic poetic is not simply to accept a different form, a pattern of sound structures and images as opposed to logically and semantically formed statements. It is also to question the very roots of making a statement about anything. The whole Imagist position becomes an attempt at avoiding a statement which assumes common values, common sentiments; it leaves instead the image open to a myriad interpretations. The aesthetic poetic thus destroys, or at the very least avoids the claim that a poet speaks for a generation or a society in a direct rationalistic manner. The images may evoke similar feelings so that the poem may eventually speak for a particular period of time, but there will certainly be no overt reference to an assumption of common values.

The aesthetic school will claim that these assumptions have been made within the 'mainstream' of Welsh poetry as

GWYN THOMAS

well as in the social ballad or occasional verse, and that they have led to the debasement of the craft of poetry until it becomes 'yet another form of direct linguistic communication'. With characteristic panache, Dafydd Elis Thomas writes in the same essay that this Eisteddfod–bred desire for clarity and an assumption of values 'is about the last hangover of philosophical rationalism and has no legitimate roots in the mainstream of the Welsh poetic achievement'. Thus poetry for the aesthetic school should be a subtly indirect exploration. It should avoid direct statements, assumptions of common values and logical processes of thought in an attempt to preserve the function of poetry as experience which cannot be transcribed through any other media. One can readily see their point, from an intellectual standpoint and a technical one. Other media, painting among them, have been forced to explore their medium as gaining knowledge above that of the camera, through the imagination. Poetry must likewise go beyond the explicit statement. Intellectually, in an age of doubt, it should also question explicitness itself and clarity as intellectually and emotionally dubious. In short, what the aesthetic school have been saying for some time is that the kind of tradition in which Gwyn Thomas writes is overworked and that we need a new line of approach.

Theoretically, this sounds a perfectly fair and commendable position. Yet what fascinates one about Gwyn Thomas's poetry is that he has made this so-called overworked strain of poetry work for him. In a much-fragmented world, he can assume a common concern for the humanistic values. He has also been able to forge a style, sometimes allusive, sometimes elaborate, but in the main a near thing to a speaking voice, angry, meditative, sympathetic. As John Gwilym Jones said of him in his Introduction to Gwyn Thomas's first volume of poems *Chwerwder yn y Ffynhonnau,* (Bitterness in the Wells) published by Gwasg

Gee in 1962: 'He does not see himself as an eccentric, individual personality searching for the essence of things but as everyman in his common search. He is one of the society of human pilgrims, voicing its communal feelings'. And again, 'Only rarely do we find the first person singular pronoun in his poetry; 'we' and 'our' dominate'. John Gwilym Jones ends this valuable introduction by hinting at a technical position which the aesthetic school would have found a corollary of the thematic standpoint: 'There is very little here of what we have come to associate with modernism'. And yet the poems work and the later poems especially satisfy a modernistic sensibility. This is no mean achievement. In fact, it seems to call into doubt whether a poetic can be outmoded or whether the style waits, like the proverbial spinster, for the right man to come along.

Not that I think Gwyn Thomas came by his style either easily or accidentally. In the course of his three books, *Chwerwder yn y Ffynhonnau* (Bitterness in the Wells) and *Y Weledigaeth Haearn* (The Iron Vision) and *Ysgyrion Gwaed* (Blood Splinters), one can trace in him the gradual discovery of the main strength of his present position - his links with his community and his ability to convey this technically in detailed observation and occasionally in direct speech. Born in Blaenau Ffestiniog, one of the main quarrying communities of North Wales, educated at the nearby University College of Bangor where he is now a Lecturer in Welsh, Gwyn Thomas has never strayed far, geographically at least, from his native community. Whereas others may have to recreate a childhood atmosphere from memory, the speech rhythms and mental attitudes of quarrying communities in the North are in the air which Gwyn Thomas breathes daily. Thus when he effects a form of osmosis to speak for the people as in 'Blaenau', the long poem in *Ysgyrion Gwaed,* or assumes that he can interpret a mental attitude as in 'Joni' *(Y Weledigaeth Haearn,* p. 32) or make a direct comment on his society in its time of transition as in 'Priodas' *(Y Weledigaeth Haearn*, p. 23), he is basing his comments on years of knowledge of one particular community's main stratum. He is as Professor Caerwyn Williams said of him in the Introduction to *Y Weledigaeth Haearn*, 'speaking as one with authority'. It is an authority which stems from a complete unself-consciousness that he is making assumptions about his fellow-men, that he is in fact daring to interpret a community to the people outside. It is a position which would make the aesthetic school shudder and it stems from a firm belief that he *does* understand this community, that he has been born into the right class of a society so that there is no alienation only firm knowledge.

It took Gwyn Thomas almost the whole of his first volume of poems *Chwerwder yn y Ffynhonnau*, to understand this strength and to use it within his verse. Many of the poems in his first collection, 'Ynysoedd Unig', 'Natur', 'Y Gerdd Ni Chenir', 'Bod', 'Crwydro', 'Môr', reflect the traditional romantic occupation of a young poet - the yearning for that which cannot be achieved, loneliness, the unending quest of life's journey, nature's hard-heartedness in the face of man's struggle, the involvement of nature in man's emotions, traditional pathetic fallacies. The language also reflects the fact that these poems have been written as it were bookishly without the full use of the creative imagination. For instance in the poem, 'Ynysoedd Unig', the second verse reflects traditionalist Romantic imagery for the island of dreams which has figured prominently in Welsh verse along with the resurgence of interest in the Arthurian legends at the turn of the century, although here the island is used as an image for the loneliness inside man's inner self:

Mae gwawn o haul yn yr awyr, a chreithiau mellt,
Ac mae glas y gwanwyn a glas y gaeaf yn y dail a'r gwellt,

Yn yr hwyr yn yr oerni asur mae gemau yng ngoleuni'r gwyll,
A chymylau cnawdol fel bwystfilod o grombil y dyfnder hyll.

(There's a gossamer sun in the heavens and scars of lightning/ The greeness of Spring and Winter is in the leaves and grass/ At the late hour in the azure coldness, jewels shine in the light of dusk/ And sensual monster clouds roll from the ugly depths).

This reflects nothing of the quality of actual observation which is to be found in passages of Gwyn Thomas's later verse, though one may argue that the imagery here is apt enough for its purpose. When the poem switches to an attempt at describing modern life, the lack of observation, the second-hand abstract quality of the language is quickly exemplified:

O balmantau dinesig ein cyfathrach, o gysur a blinder cyd-fyw,
O blith adeiladau ein diwylliant a'n diwydiant gwael a gwiw,

(From the city pavements of our daily concerns, from the comfort and tiredness of co-existence/ From the midst of the buildings of our culture and our shabby industry)

One has the feeling that the rhythm seems to dominate the lines dragging words along with it, and those words very often do not bear their full value. The early poems are riddled with abstractions, a corollary perhaps of the bookish quality of the themes and the second-hand imagery. For instance, the poem 'Crwydro' which has as its theme man's perpetual quest for meaning in life begins:

Diau y disgwyliai orfoledd wedi'r daith
Ar ol creulondeb y ffordd ddiffaith
Ond siom oedd y cwbl.

(Doubtless he expected rejoicing after his journey/ After the cruelty of the waste road, but all was disappointment).

In fairness, the second and third passages of this poem do attempt to clothe abstractions in imagery but there is no real fusion between the philosophical, rational exposition and the imagery. This failure to make the creative imagination fuse in one moment, emotion, image and the line of thought, the Eliot theory of fine verse, recurs in some of Gwyn Thomas's later poetry. For instance, when he adventurously tries his hand on a theme which is obviously strange to him as in the description of the cell/amoeba theory of creation in 'Hiliogaeth Cain' (B.B.C. Commissioned Poem in *Ysgyrion Gwaed)*. It can also lead him into rhetoric and abstraction and a rather Hebraic Psalmist parallelism and repetition, which relies heavily on the rhythm pattern without, it seems, much concentration of creativity. One example is the early poem 'Ar ôl yr Ail Ryfel Byd':

> *Wrth roi cyfnod yn y pridd mewn arch*
> *Fe dybiem ein bod yn hau gobeithion,*
> *Wrth roddi clwyfau yn y ddaear meddyliem*
> *Fod rhaid anesmwyth wedi'i dorri yn y gwraidd*
> *A bod hen fyd yn farw.*

(As we buried one era in earth in its coffin/ we believed ourselves to be planting seeds of hope/ as we put our wounds in earth we thought/ that restless necessity had been cut down by its roots/ and that the old world was dead.)

Although evidence of this slipping from concentrated writing peers through in some of Gwyn Thomas's later poems, naturally enough it is in the first volume that we find the heaviest concentration before the style matured to its later tightness. Yet in this first volume there is evidence to show that he had touched upon his sources of strength without perhaps fully realising their potential - (a poet should

171

not perhaps realise fully what roots he can tap lest he expend them and droop into facility). There are a few poems in *Chwerwder yn y Ffynhonnau* which certainly point the way to his later poetry - 'Nos Mewn Tref' is one of them. The whole poem reflects the primitive terror of nightfall and loneliness in an urban context:-

Bydd pobl mewn ceir yn dilyn goleuni ar y ffordd,
A thu hwnt i'r llewyrch bydd y nos,
Yn cilio o flaen y cerbyd am lathenni
Yna'n cau amdano.
Bydd gorsafoedd yn welw
A phobl yn gwylio'r cloc wrth ddisgwyl am drên
Yn teimlo dieithrwch uwch byrddau a chwpanau'r
rheilffyrdd
A bydd sŵn y llwyau ar y llestri'n wahanol i'r hyn ydyw yn y
dydd.

(People in cars follow lights on the road/ and beyond the glare night/ retreats for yards in front of the car/ then closes around it./ Pale railway stations/ with people watching the clock while waiting their train/ feeling the strangeness on the railway tables and cups/ and the noise of the cups and teaspoons differs from what it is in daylight)

It is a short poem, not particularly startling but the quality of the observation is exact enough to evoke enough feeling to carry us through the claims of the last four lines:

Bydd cyfnodau gwareiddiad yn cloi i'w gilydd fel
sbienddrych,
A daw anesmwythyd anelwig
Fel mwg oddi ar hen allorau
Drychiolaeth o oes yr arth a'r blaidd i ganol yr holl
beiriannau.

(The ages of civilisation lock into one another like a telescope/ and an ill-defined restlessness grows/ like smoke from the old altars/ a wraith from the stone age amidst all the modernity.)

This is one of the few poems in Gwyn Thomas's first collection which gathers its strength from exact and detailed observation of the urbanised world around him, and which gains strength from portraying an emotion which is clearly proven so that the fusion of feeling and observation is possible. 'Llofft yn Llundain' and 'Bye-Bye Love' among others, show the same tendency. In these poems, Gwyn Thomas has realised that he has a fund of experience of common life which he can use, and from now on he will use these images constantly as well as producing poems directly about an urban happening or a person within his community as in 'Dic', 'Priodas', 'Llawforwyn', 'Hen Wraig' - to name but a few in his second volume of poems.

Gwyn Thomas must have realised that his strength as an image-maker rested in references to the community he knew. He must also have discovered one other fact about his return to the known for his subject matter - a style which was to grow into his trademark as a poet. As he returned to an urban setting, to a modern 'scene' for his material, so his style quietens, becomes less bookish, less rhetorical, more the speaking voice. Slowly he becomes a master of the conversational opening which sets the scene - a quiet adequate kind of opening sometimes to match a sympathetic mood as in 'Hen Wraig':

> *Yno yn yr ystafell a'r llenni wedi·eu cau*
> *I gadw'r haul melyn ohoni, mae'r hen wraig*
> *Yn eistedd o flaen ei thân gaeafgoch*
> *A'r llwch yn crynhoi o'i hamgylch.*

(There in the room with its curtains closed/ to keep the

yellow sun out, the old woman/ sits by her winter warm fire/ while the dust settles around her.)

At other times, the opening is deliberately conversationally shocking as in 'Pethau ar eu Hanner',

> *Fe aeth carreg â hanner ei ben o*
> (A stone carried away half his head).

where the controlled flippancy of conversational manner lends authenticity to a mood which starts as a hysterical laugh and quietens to the final four lines:-

> *A minnau roeddwn i ar ganol ffrae*
> *Gydag o, am bris llefrith.*
> *Choeliech chi ddim dadleuwr mor daer o'i blaid o*
> *Ydi angau.*

(As for me, I was in the middle of an argument/ with him about the price of milk/ you'd never believe what a firm mediator on his behalf/ is death.)

When one compares these few lines, the way the poem opens dramatically and closes simply, one would not credit the fact that they had been written by the young poet who wrote 'Ynysoedd Hud'. The style has matured into simplicity, a simplicity firmly under control, linked with speech rhythms and based on an incident which is completely familiar. It seemed that Gwyn Thomas had to cut through his own learning, his own acquisition of a vocabulary from Welsh literature before he found the direct speech which would stand the test of modernity being 'yet another' form of direct statement but conveying by its rhythm, its word pattern, by its very simplicity, so much more than a line of prose.

Yet Gwyn Thomas's verse if it was to develop could not stay with the extreme, studiously casual simplicity of his second collection. By his third volume, *Ysgyrion Gwaed* he is able to bring into play a little of the richness of vocabulary of the first volume, and the control of the second; he is able to use his new-found style for observation of nature, but instead of being content with romantic description, he is by now an exacting observer. Indeed, some of his verses in the third collection like 'Octopus' and 'Môr', seem to be Rilke-like exercises in rhythm and observation. Where the strength of the richer style shows through however, is in the B.B.C. Commissioned Poem 'Blaenau' the first half of which I would consider among the very best things which Gwyn Thomas has written. The feeling for man's loneliness is here, the fear of silence of night as in the poem 'Nos Mewn Tref', but the language has gathered strength, is richer, more taut:

> *Mae sŵn llechi'n crafu'r nos*
> *Fel y daw haenfeydd y glaw o'r gorllewin*
> *I lacio'r tywyllwch a pheri i'r rwbel redeg*
> *Ar hen domen fawr chwarel yr Oclis.*

('There is the sound of slates scratching the night/ as the rain drives in from the West/ to slacken the darkness causing the rubble to run/ on the big tip of Oclis Quarry.)

The main feature about this sort of observation which he grows expert at is that it is in the long run an exploration of feeling. He certainly knows how to portray the rubble running, but the inverted verbs 'to slacken the darkness', 'scratching the night' puts the emphasis on darkness rather than on the quarry proper. Again in the description of the town itself in the second stanza, it is the smallness of the town compared with the rock, which is emphasised, and man's punniness against Nature's enduring hardness.

Ar brynhawn noeth yn y gaeaf
Fe welwch freichled o dref ar asgwrn y graig
A'r cerrig gafaelfawr yn gwyro drosti
A dynion bach ar asennau amser
Yn symud o gwmpas eu pethau.

(On a naked afternoon in winter/ you will see a bracelet of a town on the bone of rock/ and the gripping rocks bending over it/ while small men on the ribs of time/ move about their businesses.)

This sort of image-making uses the sensuous quality which marked Gwyn Thomas's early verse but uses it with the exactness and toughness which makes for the true sensuousness as distinct from sentimentality. His description of Spring and the sun drawing forth life from the rock in Blaenau is one of his finest pieces of writing, lyrical, soft and sensuous and gaining strength as relief from the hardness of the description of the first two stanzas, part of which are quoted above:

Mae ei dynerwch yn hollti'r graig ac yn malurio'r pridd
Yn llusgo pethau eiddilwyrdd—fel baglau rhedyn—
Rhwng cerrig ac yn rhoi gwe werdd o dyfiant ar wyneb y
graig.
Mae'n swil wrth anwylo blodau a sgimpen o ddaear
Ac mae ei fysead yn lliwiau i gyd ac yn beraroglau
O gyffwrdd petalau. Daw bywyd i dywallt o'r graig.

(His tenderness splits the rock and breaks up the earth/ dragging tender-green things - like fern fronds/ between rocks, giving a green web of growth on the rock surface./ It is shy while carressing flowers from a skim of earth/ and his fingers are all colours and perfume/ from touching petals. Life pours from the rock).

176

Again it is a passage of nature description and finely done
but the pathetic fallacies — used deliberately and to so much
more effect than in poems like 'Môr' in his first volume —
and the verbs used stress the emotion, the relief of tenderness
within the grim aspect of 'Blaenau' much more than the
natural phenomenon itself. I would consider this poem to be
among the very finest things which Gwyn Thomas has
written. Few things in the third volume can match it for
control and richness and for the dramatic use of the speaking
voice in dialogue. Many of the poems in *Ysgyrion Gwaed*
return to the qualities of the first volume — his literary
vocabulary, a complexity of theme, a withdrawal from that
which he knows immediately and at first hand — with a
consequent loss in his ability to fuse thought and image, an
over-apparent logical process which is not inherent in the
imagery. But 'Blaenau' retains the strength which Gwyn
Thomas found in the simple conversational style of his first
volume, while adding to it a sensuousness and a more tolerant sympathy. Most important perhaps he has retained his
major strength, his intimate knowledge of what he is talking
about. When he throws this away as in 'Hiliogaeth Cain' for
instance, the poem becomes a *tour-de-force* in allusiveness,
in dramatic ordering of verse patterns, rhythm patterns and
so on, but the immediateness of the imagery and its coupling
with the emotion is lacking and the poem shows it.

So far I have confined the analysis of Gwyn Thomas's
modernity to his ability to treat a modern theme in a social
context and to his technical ability to form conversational
patterns in his poems, which are hard-won rewards for careful pruning and real talent. But modernity is also very much
an attitude of mind and it is here that Gwyn Thomas proves
his claim to be discussed as a modern poet, although it must
be remembered that an attitude of mind clothed the wrong
way technically cannot make poetry. Probably the most
important fact about Gwyn Thomas is his ability to see con

stantly paradox in life. From his first volume to his third, we are constantly faced with opposites within one poem, and the greatest paradox of all to life, death, is very prominent, sometimes tenderly as in the descriptions of old women, sometimes shockingly as in the descriptions of road accidents, and sometimes terrifyingly menacing as in 'Yr Angau Bach'. In the midst of life we are in death, in the middle of being in one state, we find ourselves in another, this is the constant theme of Gwyn Thomas's verse. Not unnaturally it involves him in bitterness at old age since he is young, in questioning death since he is alive. More than anything it involves him in sympathy and through sympathy in anger.

Mae'r gwacter yn hel a rhagddo ni wn i ddim,
Mae tynerwch yn darfod ac ni fedraf fi ddim,
Mae bywyd yn marw ac ni allaf fi ddim

Onid efnisien ydwyf?

(The emptiness gathers and I know nothing to put against it/ tenderness dies and I can do nothing about it/ life dies and I can do nothing/ am I not efnisien?)

If one notices the opening line, 'The emptiness gathers', one finds that he has carried his paradox into his language, that in fact his language has gathered in strength precisely because he has been a good enough poet to gather the duality of life into his poems. Not all his paradoxes work when he attempts to make full poems out of them, some are too facile, some too obvious, but the attempt is seldom undertaken in a spirit of trickiness or gimmickry. This facet of his poetry underlies all which he has written and has been there from the early work such as 'Crwydro'. In fact his early romanticism is based to a large extent on this duality, but he is now treating the theme toughly rather than sentimentally, having found a means of control.

One cannot fully disentangle the weave of good poetry so

as to point out different facets standing *per se* for inspection. The duality of Gwyn Thomas is inherent in the society he was born into, in the dying nature of the quarry community in which he was brought up, in the living warmth of its people, in their poverty and tiredness and humour and perseverance, in their fatal accidents, in their old age. It is also inherent in the tenor of the times, in the transition which has happened within society from one standard of values to another, from faith to agnosticism. Gwyn Thomas's poems are largely humanistic in approach, their Christianity being mainly that of the Sermon on the Mount rather than the Resurrection. Although he would perhaps claim to be a Christian poet and has written several pieces of explicit Christian appeal, his poems generally have too much bitterness, too much sympathy, too much duality to have been written in any age except an age of doubt.

And so we end in Gwyn Thomas's beginnings. I said at the beginning of this brief analysis of the forces behind the poetry, that Gwyn Thomas knew his subject matter well and that his poetry gained in strength when he referred to the things he knew. Being a child of his time and a sensitive one, he also knew the difficulties of his time, the doubts, the transition. It is from this that he discovers the paradox in living. He is probably the first poet of his generation to try to grapple seriously, unsentimentally, with the transition to different values, to city living, to scientific thought. I do not say that he has done it successfully. The best poems, or the best parts of certain poems, still tend to be the poems where he talks of his community as he may have known it twenty years ago or may have heard about it, and they are bathed in a warmth missing from his treatment of complete modernity. There is no tenderness in his description of today, and very often he fails to change the rather flat statements into anything richer or more imaginative. The stuff of modern life as he conceives it has not penetrated into his poetry as has the sympathy and the sorrow for the washed-up communities, the old, the fatally injured or killed. Thus he is a poet of the transition era, rather than the poet of acceptance. He bases his knowledge on his locality, describing it in a style forged into a speaking voice, gaining his duality from his intimacy with the life of a few square miles, and his technical duality from a richly literary vocabulary and a simplistic dramatic sense. His importance as a poet must lie here, though I would consider him one of the most difficult of poets for the young to learn from or to emulate well. Like much good poetry, it is the achievement of finding the true man, of hitting upon what is important to him and conveying it in terms which are ultimately completely personal. Perhaps it is this comment about him more than any other which indicates my respect for the achievement within Gwyn Thomas's poetry.

A poet of transition. The stuff from which Gwyn Thomas derived much of his early images, the stuff from which 'Blaenau' was made, is no longer available. Once done, time sees to it that there is no continuation and that the modernity which Gwyn Thomas implicitly half-condemns is now here, waiting not for an expression of duality but for someone to come to terms with it. I had the feeling that Gwyn Thomas himself had realised this in *Ysgyrion Gwaed*, that in the shorter poems he was searching around for something recognisably his to deal with, without being again an expression of his society which was by now largely gone. I believe that early 1973 will see a new volume of poems. We can eagerly expect that this young poet, who has grappled with and controlled more varieties of feeling than most poets attempt in a lifetime, will find the controlled balance and richness of some of the 1965-69 poems in a new theme. Certainly his past poems suggest that he is capable of change and development. More so than most perhaps. It is a task

which he set himself fairly early on: in a poem entitled
'Lliwiau':

> *Wrth dyfu o fachgendod mae dyn yn teimlo*
> *Amser yn araf bach yn dod i afael ynddo.*
> *Mae'r corff sydd yn cynnal byw*
> *Y ffenestr eglur ar y byd yn newid*
> *Ac mae'r cof, yn ddarluniau a gasglwyd*
> *Yn dechrau cronni a hel ei liwiau hydddi*
>
> *Oni bydd ffrwydro rhyw fiwsig yn y galon*
> *I lanhau i weledigaeth newydd*
> *Y mae un yn troi tua'r bedd wedi'i gloi*
> *Y tu ôl i hen liwiau.*

(As he grows from boyhood a man senses/ time slowly
gaining its hold on him/ The body which supports life/ the
clear window on the world, changes/ and memory with the
pictures it collects/ starts gathering and spreading its
colours over it.
Unless there is an explosion of music in the heart/ to cleanse
it to a new vision/ one will turn towards death locked away/
behind the old colours).

This is the hardest of tasks as one grows older, the kind of
task which separates the young versifier from those who constantly, through hard struggle, recreate themselves in their
maturity. I believe that some of Gwyn Thomas's past poetry
has shown him capable of re-creation so that he can cleanse
our own faded vision and lend us new colours.